Learning from Pictures

BY CATHARINE M. WILLIAMS ■ ASSOCIATE

PROFESSOR, COLLEGE OF EDUCATION ■ THE

OHIO STATE UNIVERSITY ■ COLUMBUS, OHIO

■ PUBLISHED BY THE DEPARTMENT OF AUDIO-

VISUAL INSTRUCTION ■ NATIONAL EDUCATION

ASSOCIATION ■ 1201 SIXTEENTH STREET,

N.W., WASHINGTON 6, D.C.

Copyright 1963

Department of Audiovisual Instruction

National Education Association

Library of Congress

Catalog Card Number: 63-15331

Single copy, $4.50. Quantity orders at the
following discounts: 2-9 copies, 10 percent;
10 or more copies, 20 percent. Order from
and make checks payable to the National
Education Association, 1201 Sixteenth Street,
N.W., Washington 6, D.C.

Contents

Preface

This book is intended for teachers. It comes at a time when there is great interest in the technological revolution taking place in our society and in our schools. It comes at a time when there are more students than ever before who must learn more and more in less and less time. It comes at a time when school administrators, audiovisual directors, and librarians are—more than ever before—in a position to supply teachers with an increasing variety of instructional tools, including tremendous picture resources.

Dr. Williams has done a great service to American education in writing the text as well as in compiling the Primary Source List (see page 125) and the Subject Index (see page 147). The Department of Audiovisual Instruction is proud to publish this important work.

Readers and producers of picture materials are invited to assist us in keeping the Primary Source List current for future editions of this work and for supplements that may be issued from time to time. Please send your suggestions to the Department of Audiovisual Instruction, 1201 Sixteenth Street, N.W., Washington 6, D.C.

The Department of Audiovisual Instruction

Acknowledgments

The author is deeply indebted to many teachers, who have been enrolled in her classes and workshops, for suggestions on specific uses of pictures which they have contributed from their teaching experience. To make specific acknowledgment would be impossible.

To Wanda Daniels Domino special acknowledgment is due. Publication of a volume of this sort was originally suggested by her when she was Wanda Daniels, director of Audio-Visual Services, Grosse Pointe, Michigan, Public Schools. As chairman of the DAVI Committee on Instructional Materials, no longer in existence, she named Mildred Ellzey, a teacher from Austin, Texas, to give leadership to the project. Just when the project got under way, Miss Ellzey married and gave up her professional activities. Soon thereafter the Committee was dissolved and the project laid aside. At Mrs. Domino's instigation plans for the book were reconsidered, and the author was asked to prepare it.

Both Mrs. Domino and the author recognize that the compilation of a source listing of pictorial materials, as complete and up to date as is needed by teachers, could not be accomplished on the first attempt. Therefore, the Primary Source List contained in this book was prepared with the understanding that the Department of Audiovisual Instruction would actively seek the cooperation of audiovisual directors, teachers, publishers, and everyone else interested in instructional pictures for suggestions and information regarding good teaching pictures.

In the writing of certain sections of this volume, the author has drawn on special materials generously contributed by three colleagues in the audiovisual field: she expresses appreciation to Margaret W. Divizia, administrator, Instructional Aids and Services Branch, Los Angeles City Schools, for her contribution, "Materials Produced by School Systems," beginning on page 107; to Marjorie East, head, Home Economics Education, Pennsylvania State University, for help concerning the use of pictorial materials in "Home Economics," beginning on page 67; and to Margaret D. Saylor, director of Visual Education and Safety, the Parma, Ohio, Public Schools, for having so freely shared with us her experience in working with community groups to improve instruction, page 123.

Special thanks are recorded here to those public schools and other organizations which so generously made their picture files available as this book was being prepared. These groups include the NEA Journal, the Publications Division of the NEA, the Standard Oil Company of New Jersey, the United Nations, and the United Nations Educational, Scientific, and Cultural Organization.

Also, thanks are due to the many publishers of pictures for their fine response to requests for samples and information about their materials.

The author expresses special appreciation to Robert W. O'Leary of the NEA staff for his imaginative design and thoughtful layout of the book.

A final word of thanks is due Dr. Robert C. Snider of the DAVI staff for his invaluable help not only in preparing the manuscript for press but also for furnishing many suggestions for its improvement.

C.M.W.

Columbus, Ohio
March 1963

Learning from Pictures

Choosing Pictures

Flat pictures are the oldest, the least expensive, and the most universally available of all materials of instruction. Used either alone or in conjunction with other curriculum materials, good pictures *can* help to make learning an interesting adventure in living. Whether or not pictures used as teaching tools actually *do* contribute richly to the learning process depends upon how the teacher structures the learning situation. For instance, it is possible to structure the situation so that it requires any one of these three responses: (a) recitation of facts, (b) facsimile of what was presented, (c) creative thinking (either alone or as active members of a cooperating group)— making extensive use of newly acquired facts and ideas in the process.

The teacher who structures the situation in either of the first two ways will discover but few needs for pictures. In these classroom situations, emphasis is placed on *knowing about* things rather than on *knowing* them; on relating new information to the responses the child has learned to make rather than to what he actually knows. The teacher is not much concerned about how the child "sees" things because she is so engrossed in telling him how he "should see" them or in hearing him tell her what the book says.

When pictures are selected and used to achieve the teaching goals indicated here, they will be limited to those which reinforce or illustrate the textbook; they will seldom be used to add new dimensions to the learning. Concerned with answers rather than with interpretations, the teacher will present the picture and point out what she considers noteworthy, rather than draw out from children what the picture "means" to them. Pictures will be used to define and set limits rather than to serve as bridges to new relationships. In these classrooms, picture displays are more likely to be arranged for purposes of decoration than for learning. A display may decorate the

TO DEVELOP CREATIVE THINKING, STUDENTS NEED HELP IN PERCEIVING
AND TRANSLATING THEIR NEW-FOUND KNOWLEDGE INTO BEHAVIOR.
(PHOTO: STANDARD OIL CO., N.J.)

room for an entire month during which time it may be referred to only
casually, if at all.

Pictures that children make will be characterized by their similarities rather than by their differences. Children will be encouraged to
copy and trace rather than to express what they see, feel, and think.
In short, their pictures are not used as a means of communication.

PICTURES AID LEARNING

The teacher who structures the situation so that it requires the
third response, creative thinking, conceives her own role as guidance
directed at helping students to perceive and then to translate their
new-found knowledge into behavior.

To help students think creatively, the teacher must be concerned
with learning what beliefs they hold. She understands that whether
one's beliefs are based on valid assumptions, experimental data, and
knowledge or on half-truths, superstition, and false impressions, they
represent reality to the individual. For example, in a family where
there are two girls and a boy, "the new baby in our household" might
be perceived differently by each child. The youngest child might

"see" this baby as stealing coveted parental attention; the boy might "see" the new baby as a buddy, a man-child ally; the older sister might "see" him as a live doll responsive to her "mothering."

Because behavior with reference to any idea, object, or situation is governed by the way the particular thing in question is perceived, each of these children will behave differently with reference not only to the baby but to the new situation at home.

Let us suppose that the child who perceived the baby as a threat is a seven-year-old girl in our teacher's second grade. Were the parents to turn to this teacher for guidance, she would point out how differences in behavior of their three children were directly traceable to differences in the way the three children perceived the situation— the new baby in our household. By reviewing together the three children's past experiences, they could see their role in perception. As related past experiences, both older children had experienced "a new baby" with no unhappy associations, and both had experienced wishing—wishing for a brother; wishing for a lifelike doll. For the youngest child, this new baby was an entirely new experience, one in which someone else bore the title "our baby," the title by which she had always been introduced by her parents. Next the teacher would make it quite clear that, to bring about desirable changes in behavior, it is necessary to bring about a change in the way the situation is perceived. No doubt, she would tactfully suggest ways in which the parents could help their daughter to discover that the baby created no change in their relationships with her.

For the sake of illustration, let us assume also that the teacher decided to create some classroom situations to relate the new baby to some interesting new knowledge. Her plans might include encouraging all of her pupils to bring pictures of baby brothers, baby sisters, or baby friends for sharing. The teacher might direct discussion and the *reading* of these pictures, and of others which she supplied, toward learning what activities indicated different stages of development. By this procedure, the teacher would be starting where the seven-year-old child was and focusing attention on a baby in a particular relation to her, that is, as someone interesting to observe because his actions might be anticipated and noted.

This hypothetical classroom situation not only demonstrates ways in which a single child's perception might be changed but also shows how skillful teachers work to develop concepts. Note that by having children contribute pictures and relate their own observations to these pictures, the teacher would be able to gauge where each child was in relation to his understanding of such things as care of babies and activities typical of babies at various stages of their development. With this information, the teacher would be equipped to help every child in the class relate his new knowledge to that which he already possessed.

Had she launched such an activity, her planning might well have included a way of making the term "stages of development" meaningful. For example, use of pictures of the lima bean, from planting date to leafy seedling, followed by children's planting a number of bean seeds and keeping documentary records on every seed would lead to the discovery that, while all seedlings went through the same stages, few of them reached a given stage at the same time. By analogy, then, her pupils could be helped to assume that perhaps babies, too, would not all reach a specific stage of development—turning over, sitting alone, crawling—at the same age. They could be encouraged to gather data to test this assumption.

Because these children would have no opportunities in the classroom to make use of their new knowledge, the teacher might have thought to enlist the cooperation of parents. She might have indicated how she was using their homes as rich laboratory resources and how reports (both pictorial and verbal) of children's "laboratory" observations and experiences were promoting learning. It is probable, too, that she would have initiated, in planning with parents, ways in which she and they might more effectively work together to achieve desirable learning outcomes.

In classrooms structured for a creative approach to learning such as the one just described, pictures for study are conceived as basic materials of instruction integral to the learning situation. It is recognized that—

1. Pictures can make a unique contribution to learning.
2. Some people learn more readily from one medium than from another (so more than one medium is provided).
3. Through activities such as selecting and using pictures for their own purposes—for example, a report, a unit of study, a display arrangement—pupils learn to discriminate, to be resourceful, and to assume and carry through responsibilities.

To utilize picture resources for creative learning, guidance will be directed at helping children learn not only to "read" pictures but also

THOUGHTFUL SELECTION OF PICTURES
BECOMES A REALITY ONLY
WHEN THE TEACHER FINDS HERSELF
IN A POSITION TO COMPARE AND
CHOOSE FROM A COLLECTION THAT
HAS ALREADY BEEN CAREFULLY
BUILT UP OVER THE YEARS.
(PHOTO: UNIVERSITY SCHOOL,
OHIO STATE UNIVERSITY)

to read pictures at increasingly higher levels. Also, it will be directed at providing numerous opportunities for children to use pictures (both their own productions and their own selections) and other resources for achieving their purposes in as independent a fashion as they are able. Obviously when children produce pictures, each for his own purposes, the pictures will have individuality, for they will express the ideas, feelings, and thinking of the individual.

In these classrooms the picture materials will not be considered exclusively as the teacher's resources; they will be "our pictures." Pupils as well as teachers will feel responsible for adding to the collection such pictures as are especially pertinent. The files will be organized in such a way that the pupils can readily locate pictures for their own use. In these classrooms pictures will be used to serve a variety of purposes.

INSTRUCTIONAL PURPOSES
SERVED BY PICTURES

Recall Experiences

As she helps young children to express themselves freely and to develop readiness for reading, the teacher capitalizes on what is familiar. She selects pictures of children's everyday activities to help her pupils recall their own related experiences.

Aid Detailed Study

Air views, close-ups, diagrams, magnifications, reduced images, and X-ray prints make possible detailed study of subjects which otherwise would be impossible.

THE CAMERA BRINGS FARAWAY PLACES INTO THE CLASSROOM SO THAT
THEY ARE NEITHER AS REMOTE NOR AS DIFFERENT IN TIME AND SPACE
AS THEY ONCE WERE. THIS STUDY IN CONTRAST SHOWS THE NEW
STATE LIBRARY IN ACCRA, GHANA, AND PROVIDES THE BASIS FOR
TEACHING SOME IMPORTANT INFORMATION ABOUT THIS REGION.
(PHOTO: UNITED NATIONS)

Correct Misconceptions

Because children's concepts are frequently formed on the basis of
limited experience or faulty interpretation of verbal explanation, they
develop misconceptions which they hold, sometimes, for years. Pictures, carefully selected, can be powerful aids for correcting false
impressions. If a child believes, for example, that *all* Africans live
primitively and savagely, pictures of life in cities will help him to
recognize that only *some* Africans live in an undeveloped society.

Prevent Misconceptions

The wise teacher anticipates concepts and terminology that may not be clearly understood without visual imagery and supplies pictures to help understanding. For example, when a child first hears the word *seahorse*, to describe a species of small fish, he will be confused—already familiar with the word *horse* as designating a well-known hoofed quadruped—unless he is shown a picture of this new *horse*.

Compare and Contrast

When two or more pictures of comparable objects are placed side by side, study of the pictures makes possible identification of similarities and differences between the objects. Pictures also permit comparison of items too delicate to withstand the handling close examination would require.

Build New Experiences

Often, horizons must be extended by vicarious rather than by firsthand experiences. For example, when a place as remote as ancient Egypt is studied, a set of study prints best helps the learners to visualize and understand early Egyptian civilization.

PICTURES SUCH AS THIS ARE ESSENTIAL FOR PREVENTING MISCONCEPTIONS AND LEARNING ABOUT EVENTS THAT ARE ALMOST COMPLETELY REMOVED FROM THE EXPERIENCE OF TODAY'S CHILDREN. HOW DO THESE CONSTRUCTION METHODS AND SOURCES OF POWER COMPARE WITH THOSE OF TODAY? (PHOTO: INFORMATIVE CLASSROOM PICTURES)

BUILDING A PYRAMID IN EGYPT
INFORMATIVE CLASSROOM PICTURE SERIES
Plate 5 — Early Civilization
Copyright I.C.P.A.

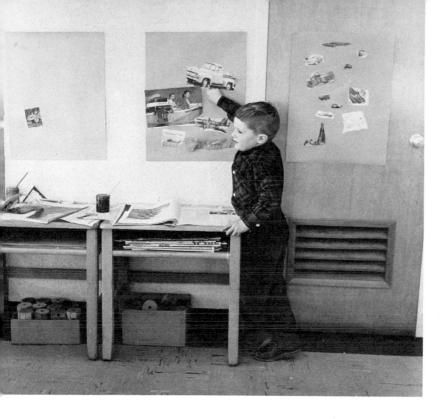

Give Meaning to Word Symbols

A picture and a brief explanation can make even the most difficult word a meaningful part of a child's vocabulary. Consider how much easier explaining aqueduct, blockhouse, combine, sextant, or zebra would be with the aid of a picture. Specialized vocabulary for a topic of study is often more readily mastered when a group makes its own picture dictionary.

Demonstrate a Process

By means of pictures, it is possible to present, a step at a time, in proper sequence, all stages in a how-to-do-it procedure—for example, linoleum block printing—and all phases of a developmental process—for example, the embryonic development of a chick. Discussion completed, the pictures serve for easy summary and review; when displayed, they provide an excellent reference for students until they have mastered each procedure.

Form Value Judgments

Pictures play a major role in propaganda techniques. Through guided picture study students can learn to search for facts, to recognize half-truths and misleading information, and to acquire the ability to form value judgments. By studying the dramatic appeal of illustrated posters issued for fund-raising campaigns, students will become aware of the motivation behind the pictures. For example, by studying the dramatic appeal of illustrated advertisements, along with the accompanying text, students will discover their underlying assumptions and anticipate the conclusions unwary consumers are likely to reach.

Create an Atmosphere

Pictures can turn a drab classroom into an attractive setting: a colorful textile print of performing circus animals for a kindergarten room; a wall hanging on which fourth-grade children have impressed block prints of their favorite book characters for a reading corner; or, for a sixth-grade class studying the country, travel posters on Switzerland.

Prepare for Further Experience

In preparation for a study trip, a laboratory experiment, or a complicated demonstration, pictures may be used to sharpen insights and focus attention on what to look for and how to look for it.

BEFORE VISITING THE MUSEUM, STUDENTS WILL GAIN MUCH USEFUL INFORMATION FROM STUDY PRINTS SUCH AS THIS ONE, FURNISHED TO LOCAL SCHOOLS BY THE LOS ANGELES COUNTY MUSEUM.

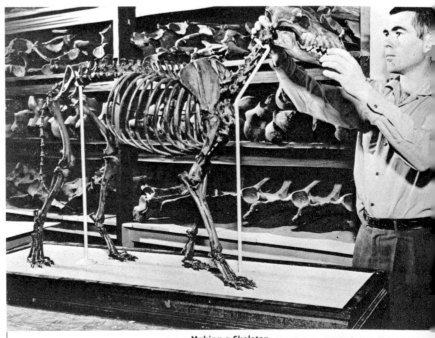

Making a Skeleton

This man is making a skeleton of a Dire Wolf. He has used bones from many Dire Wolves. He made a plastic bone when he could not find the real bone. He put the bones where they grew in a wolf's body.

He made a hole in each one and put it on a wire form. It takes a long time to make a skeleton.

L.A. City Schools 75-Picture courtesy L.A. County Museum
THE LA BREA TAR PITS OF HANCOCK PARK   1   500   **8**

LEARNING WITHOUT INTEREST
IS STERILE, BUT LEARNING
BASED ON SOUND MOTIVATION
OFTEN CANNOT BE STOPPED.
HERE A TEACHER USES PICTURES
TO INTEREST STUDENTS
IN A FORTHCOMING SCIENCE UNIT.
(PHOTO: SAN DIEGO
(CALIF.) CITY SCHOOLS)

Motivate Learning

Introduction of pictures can motivate learning, especially if the teacher provides time for reading and discussion to build awareness of differences in interpretation among themselves and to raise questions suggested by the pictures.

Publicize Events

Pictures can arouse interest in both current and forthcoming events. The opening of a local zoo, the inauguration of a president, or the completion of a bridge becomes meaningful for children when they have seen pictures of the events.

Develop Insight and Appreciation

By evoking emotional responses, pictures can develop in children greater appreciation of life around them. The artist and the camera can record scenes which children would never see or, without assistance from the teacher, never fully appreciate: the awesomeness of the Grand Canyon, the joy of a child at a circus, the grimness of a tenement, the horror of war.

Dramatize a Point

A cleverly dramatized point is usually a point well made and long remembered. An English teacher sketched a single hat stretched across three heads to illustrate the faulty use of pronouns in a student's sentence, "Each of the three boys wore *their* hat." Then, he drew another sketch showing each boy wearing a different hat. The two pictures convinced the class that, for the sake of common sense, the sentence must read, "Each of the three boys wore *his* hat."

Raise Questions and Present Problems

A teacher can start a good discussion by presenting a picture and asking such questions as "What is the problem presented in this picture?" and "Do the measures taken in this picture indicate a solution to the underlying problem?" Pictures used as the basis for discussion encourage young people to think critically, observe carefully, and question intelligently.

Stimulate Reading

Pictures can arouse enough interest in a specific story, object, or subject that, in order to satisfy their curiosity, boys and girls will explore whatever library facilities the school and community offer.

FEW COMMUNICATIONS DEVICES IN OUR SOCIETY ARE AS EFFECTIVE AS THE CAPTIONED DRAWING IN ITS MANY MANIFESTATIONS— AS POLITICAL CARTOONS, ADVERTISEMENTS, AND, MORE RECENTLY, AS ADULT "COLORING BOOKS."

ELEMENTARY CLASSROOM WALLS OFTEN TELL MUCH ABOUT CURRENT LEARNING ACTIVITIES IN A SCHOOL AND PROVIDE A VISUAL FRAMEWORK FOR MANY KINDS OF STUDENT ACTIVITY. (PHOTO: CLEVELAND PUBLIC SCHOOLS)

Foster Individual Interest

Many a child has been encouraged by pictures thoughtfully provided for his use by a teacher who "remembered" his personal interest or ambition. Opportunity to browse through a picture collection is especially valuable for children who have meager picture resources at home. Such an opportunity may lead a child to discover a special area of interest.

Provide Setting

Pictures can provide the setting and background needed by a reader for full appreciation of an historical novel, a book on world travel, or a factual account of a technical experiment.

Complete Research

Pictures and reading matter supplement each other so well that without both research is incomplete. A pictorial record documents findings and supplements a written account.

Provide Reference

Well-selected pictures are invaluable guides for preparing scenery and costumes for an historical play, an international festival, or a mural.

REPORTING A RECENT TRIP, REAL OR IMAGINARY, MIGHT BE DULL FOR ALL CONCERNED IF IT WEREN'T ENLIVENED WITH ILLUSTRATIONS. (PHOTOS: LEFT, OHIO STATE UNIVERSITY; RIGHT, CLEVELAND PUBLIC SCHOOLS)

Enrich and Enliven Reports

To make an effective presentation before his classmates—for his own growth and for the benefit of his listeners—the student inexperienced in public speaking should employ every resource at his command. Teachers, therefore, should guide activities so that students use pictures in the preparation and presentation of reports. For example, an eighth grader's use of his own sketches during a talk on the beaks and claws of birds served to hold the attention of his classmates.

Invite Participation

Displays addressed to the viewers often encourage them to participate in an activity. For example, pictures of important steps in the process of linoleum block printings, with wall hangings, yearbook illustrations, and greeting cards of block prints as samples, brought requests to learn the process.

Help Learners Understand Themselves

Pictures showing attitudes, behavior patterns, and problems of teen-agers are not too difficult to find. Such pictures help students realize that the problems which trouble them are not unique. They also provide situations for discussion without the embarrassment of personal identification.

Build Background

Often both the meaning and significance of a potentially valuable experience are lost to the learner because no one has had the foresight to build the background essential for understanding. For instance, to appreciate the word pictures in the poem "The Chambered Nautilus," one needs to have seen a picture of a cross section of the nautilus shell if he has never seen the object itself.

Create Centers of Interest

A few carefully selected items combined with a few well-chosen pictures can be used to create conversation pieces. For example, a few book jackets, a reproduction of an artist's sketch, several textile prints, and a horse-head walking stick, arranged in a corridor display case, started comments which led a number of students to discover that they shared an interest in horses.

PICTURES, BOOKS, AND OBJECTS CAN OFTEN BE RELATED TO HEIGHTEN INTEREST IN A PARTICULAR SUBJECT, AND PUPILS WHO HAVE RESPONSIBILITY FOR SUCH DISPLAYS OFTEN DEVELOP A CONTAGIOUS ENTHUSIASM. (PHOTO: OHIO STATE UNIVERSITY)

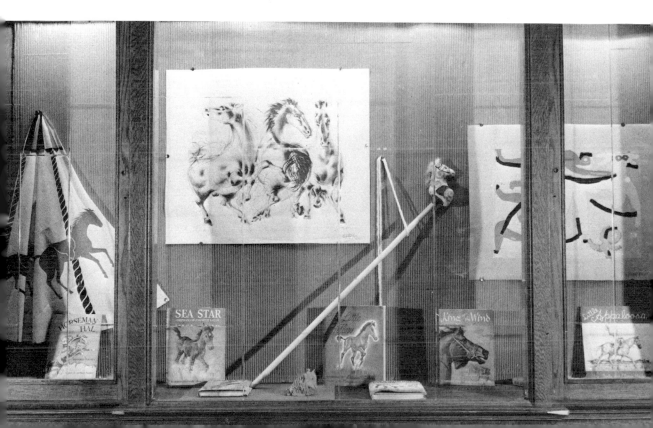

VISUAL LITERACY
CAN BEST BE DEVELOPED
WHEN PUPILS HAVE OPPORTUNITY
AND RESPONSIBILITY
FOR USING PICTURES TO ACHIEVE
SPECIFIC COMMUNICATIONS
OBJECTIVES.
(PHOTO: OHIO STATE UNIVERSITY)

Develop Critical Judgment

When committees are given opportunity and responsibility for selecting pictures pertinent to a unit of study, the teacher can guide and develop critical judgment. Such judgment is further developed if students assume responsibility for selecting, from among the pictures which they have used in the course of a special study, those which present a point of view, develop a sequence, convey impressions consistent with one another, and the like.

Stimulate Creative Effort

Sometimes a picture supplies the imagination with the germ of an idea which the student develops into a song, a poem, a story, or another picture. For example, a picture that showed a circus poster in the background and in the foreground a boy around 10 years of age trying to walk a tightrope was one of several used by a teacher to stimulate the creative written expression of 10-year-olds.

Introduce a Topic of Study

Well-chosen pictures may be used effectively to launch a new topic. For example, a teacher of dramatics used several still close-up shots selected from sequences of outstanding films to introduce a study of how to make facial expression carry part of the burden of communication.

Review and Summarize

Pictures are uniquely suited for summary and review. The same picture that aided in initial learning will help in recall and contribute even more richly to the learning than it did at first, for in review the learner brings more to the viewing than he did in the initial study. Sometimes the teacher asks students to select a limited number of pictures which represent key ideas or to arrange them to show the sequential steps in a process.

Test Learning

Pictures can add interest and variety to a test situation and provide a reliable means of gauging mastery of subject matter. For example, a student may be tested on his ability to make practical application of the information contained in a display on petroleum.

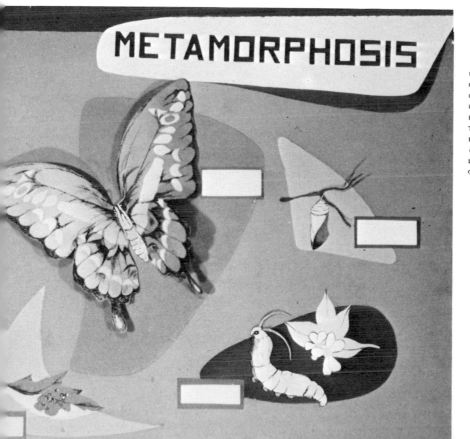

METAMORPHOSIS

UNIQUE AND OFTEN VERY RELIABLE TESTS CAN BE DEVELOPED USING PICTURE MATERIALS. HERE PUPILS ARE ASKED TO IDENTIFY VARIOUS CHANGES IN A BIOLOGICAL PROCESS. (PHOTO: TEACHING AIDS LABORATORY, OHIO STATE UNIVERSITY)

CHARACTERISTICS OF GOOD INSTRUCTIONAL PICTURES

The teacher who uses pictures effectively for instructional purposes is concerned with the quality of the pictures. A picture acceptable for educational use should—

Focus Sharply

Misty and fuzzy pictures have as little place in study sessions as do mumbled explanations. Whether a picture is in color or black and white, nothing short of a sharp print is acceptable when the primary purpose is to inform; such detail as properly belongs in a picture should be easily discernible. (This is not to say that some softness of focus is not permissible when the purpose of the picture is to establish a mood.) Sharp focus is determined, in part, by the type of paper on which the picture is printed. A hard-surface, glossy paper brings out details. A soft, dull paper will make details seem blurred and contrasts of dark and light less striking.

Present a Unified Arrangement

A picture is good when the artist, no matter in what medium he works, conveys his message to the viewer. Although the effect achieved may be neither pleasing nor pretty, the over-all composition of a good picture does have unity. The arrangement of objects, the choice of color, and the lighting have been coordinated to make one idea dominant. Even the blank spaces are an effective part of the scheme. All objects are essential and integral to the picture, and nothing appears crowded or out of place.

The person inexperienced in judging pictures for teaching purposes may feel inadequate because he has had little art education. But one need not be an artist to recognize that composition is the most essential element in a picture. In viewing the well-composed picture, the eye usually halts repeatedly at the same point—the center of interest. On the other hand, if the viewer's eye is not quickly drawn to any particular part, the picture is probably so poorly composed that the dominant idea is vague.

Convey Authentic and Truthful Impressions

Because pictures are such powerful tools of communication, it is important that those used for instructional purposes do not mislead.

Frequently, the unusual picture creates or perpetuates a misconception. Though peoples living in Arctic regions seldom occupy igloos, overuse of pictures of Eskimo igloos has led many children to believe the igloo to be a typical dwelling in these regions. Such misconceptions have their foundation in fact; they are an outgrowth of generalizations based on impressions from pictures showing the unusual rather than the typical. However, the unusual picture does have a place in a collection if it is carefully supplemented by the typical and clearly identified as being unique.

Pictures specially planned for propaganda purposes, on the other hand, should not be a part of a circulating collection, but should be reserved for special guided study. Students can understand the purpose of these pictures and develop discrimination in viewing only when they study them along with the written word—the text of advertising copy with the pictorial portion, brochures of the chamber of commerce with a picture of new industry in a town, background news stories with an editorial cartoon. It is important for the teacher to guide a class in this study so that students will be equipped to make value judgments on the pictures which play so great a role in molding opinion.

WELL-COMPOSED, WELL-REPRODUCED PICTURES THAT ARE HONEST STATEMENTS ABOUT SOME ASPECT OF LIFE ARE IMPORTANT TOOLS FOR THE CREATIVE TEACHER. (PHOTO: UNITED NATIONS)

Reproduce Color Accurately

When a picture is used to inform, it is not enough that the colors be pleasing and harmonious; the original colors should be accurately and vividly reproduced. Unnatural color produces distorted effects which are likely to mislead. Color poor in quality offends the sensitive viewer and prevents the development of good taste by the less sensitive.

Only in the case of an impressionistic picture is the naturalness of color not a consideration. Here, the artist is using color as a means of self-expression—his emotions in response to the objects he portrays. Impressionistic pictures have a place in the school collection, but it should be remembered that they are helpful in understanding and interpreting feelings and attitudes rather than in developing informational concepts.

Include Suitable Caption

A teacher must decide what caption, if any, is most suitable for the study purpose in mind. Except when used to stimulate creative expression, to promote critical thinking, or to test learning, a picture should be accompanied by a caption—a statement in sentence form calculated to stimulate interest and add to understanding. If an acceptable caption does not accompany a picture, one should be supplied by the teacher.

The caption, "The 'Island Queen' makes a record run," is sufficient for a news photograph, but inadequate for a picture filed for study purposes. The addition of a few background facts may make yesterday's news picture of value for reference purposes later. The brief caption, "A girl wears a festival costume," may be adequate for a picture which is part of a series on Brittany. Separated from the set, however, the picture will become worthless for study purposes because there is no way of placing it.

If a caption is short, teachers prefer to place it directly below the picture. If a caption provides considerable information, it is usually placed on the back of the mount to avoid spoiling the appearance of the picture and to make it easily adaptable to different uses. Take, for example, a picture of San Francisco's Golden Gate Bridge. Attached to it is information about the builder, the dimensions of the structure, and the materials used in construction. The picture may be used as a landmark in the study of California; as a study, with the Statue of Liberty, of gateways to our continent; or as an example of a specific type of bridge. In none of these cases would all of the attached information be pertinent. A brief caption below the picture would suffice. However, placed on the back of the mount, the more detailed information would be ready for use if the picture of the bridge is displayed as an example of an engineering masterpiece.

Contain Aids to Interpretation

A good picture, like a good explanation, is simple and easy to interpret. Special devices for attracting attention to key points and cues for establishing size and function help in interpretation.

When color is used as a key to parts of a picture of a complicated machine or to special features of a chart or diagram, the picture loses its effectiveness if the key contains so many colors that it is difficult to follow or if the colors are not readily distinguishable. It is wise to avoid use of red and green as "keys" in the same picture because those afflicted with red-green color blindness cannot distinguish between them.

Every picture should contain at least one object so familiar to the viewer that it can serve as a means for judging the size or purpose of unfamiliar objects. A human figure standing beside an architectural

A WEAKNESS COMMON TO MANY INSTRUCTIONAL PICTURES IS THAT THEY OFTEN CONTAIN NO INDICATION OF THE SIZE OF UNKNOWN OBJECTS. HERE THE CANCER CRAB IS RELATED TO THE FAMILIAR NICKEL. (PHOTO: FILMSCOPE, INC.)

CANCER CRAB

The five cent coin helps to show the size of the crab. When full-grown, cancer crabs are larger than striped shore crabs. They live in deeper water farther out in the tide pool. If taken from the water they bubble and snap. Cancer crabs have a hard shell which protects the tail tucked up under it. They have ten jointed legs of which the first two end in claws. Cancer crabs have a light undersurface with red spots.

FILMSCOPE INC.

fused or misled by the fact that the little girl in the foreground is several times larger than the policeman in the middle distance. Without these and many similar or related techniques, he could not grasp the import of even the simplest picture.[1]

[1] Bartlett, Mary M. *How To Teach with Pictures.* Grand Rapids, Mich.: Informative Classroom Picture Publishers, 1947. p. 12-14.

Just as there are several stages of development in reading the printed word, there are several levels of response in picture interpretation:

1. Naming objects
2. Grasping import
3. Observing detail
4. Relating the picture to experience
5. Drawing inferences
6. Adding imaginative elements
7. Engaging in further activities suggested by the pictures.[2]

Familiarity with these levels enables the teacher to gauge the extent of a child's picture-reading ability and to know the level toward which he should move.

The more practice students have interpreting pictures, the greater will be their improvement in drawing inferences. The wise teacher will ask questions to stimulate and guide the inferring process and encourage her class to observe and to inquire as well as to answer. For example, a child, on seeing a picture of a Danish church, commented, "What a steep slope to the roof!" The teacher immediately asked, "Do you recall seeing such steep buildings in pictures of any other country we have studied?" The class realized that all the countries they knew of with houses having steep-sloped roofs were located in the North. This discovery led them to the conclusion that roofs serve a functional purpose in countries with heavy snowfalls. If teachers work at providing this sort of directed observation, children will learn to use prior experience and knowledge to assist them in picture interpretation.

Children must become aware of the limitations of pictures. A picture carries only such information as the artist or photographer chooses to include. Though this may be advantageous—for he may have taken great care to make his picture a typical representation— he may have avoided the typical in order to achieve a particular effect. For example, if the photographer attempts to show housing in a particular city, he has not done an adequate job if he has overlooked the slums and the low-cost housing projects and has included only the showplaces. Children must be made aware of the danger in generalizing from a single picture when there is likelihood that it carries only part of the story.

---

[2] *Ibid.,* p. 19.

THE INTERPRETATION OF
PICTURE SYMBOLS MUST BEGIN
WITH NAMING OBJECTS FOUND
IN THE PICTURE TO BE STUDIED.
HERE A TEACHER CAREFULLY
EXPLAINS ANIMAL SILHOUETTES
FOUND IN THE MURAL.
(PHOTO: UNITED NATIONS)

Communication may break down with pictures as well as with words. Everyone knows how misunderstanding and confusion arise when words do not carry the same connotation for speaker and listener. While the language of pictures may be more universal, it, too, contains symbols which individuals can interpret differently.

Teachers will be especially alert to picture symbols which may be interpreted according to national custom or religious beliefs. They must also keep in mind that family status, personal feelings, and group identification can influence picture interpretation. It is the teachers' responsibility to recognize and clarify the significance of picture symbols which may be confusing, just as it is their responsibility to clarify difficult passages in reading. And, finally, they will help students discover exactly what factors influence their interpretation of picture symbols.

Pictorial aids alone cannot carry the burden of communication any more than words alone. Once the teacher recognizes that communication is a difficult task, she will plan to use pictorial materials and words as instruments of communication to supplement each other. She will select her picture materials with as much thoughtful consideration as she does her informational reading matter; she will assign picture references just as she does text references.

Timing in showing a picture greatly influences its effectiveness. The teacher who plans for a picture to serve a particular purpose will not be tempted to show it too soon. She will introduce each picture verbally, include at least one thought-provoking question, and provide time to observe, discover, think, question, and discuss. A picture worth using is well worth the time needed for reading and interpretation.

MAKING FULL USE OF
TEXTBOOK ILLUSTRATIONS

Judging by the textbooks coming off the press today, the value of illustrations has been widely recognized. Some textbooks are so well illustrated that adults who see them often wish that such books had been available when they were in school. In some of these textbooks, however, illustrations seem to be included only to arouse interest in the book rather than to contribute significantly to the understanding of content.

In the well-illustrated textbook, pictorial material is an integral part of the written content and is placed as close as possible to the text with which it is associated. Since the value of the pictorial materials in textbooks can be appreciated only when the illustrations are studied along with associated portions of the written text, illustrative materials should be made as much a part of the assignment as the written text; they should be discussed in class, and students should be tested on comprehension of the ideas expressed in pictures just as they are tested on ideas expressed in words.

In well-illustrated books, pictures are reproduced so that line, color, and form are sharply defined. Illustrations are captioned to help the learner with his interpretation. In the good illustration, irrelevant material has been omitted so that nothing distracts from the main idea. The illustration deals directly with the problem or issue under consideration and serves to create interest, to introduce a problem or topic, to stimulate thinking, to provoke discussion, to accent an important point, to clarify or amplify a concept, to facilitate summary, or to aid review.

At this point, an examination of a good textbook illustration to see how the teacher could make wise use of it would be valuable. The reproduction shown on page 29 is in a textbook account of Pizarro's conquest of Peru. For example, a teacher may decide to use this reproduction as an introduction to the story of Inca civilization. When she makes the assignment, the teacher will ask the class to study the picture together to see what they can discover about the Incas. She may hear such comments as "They knew how to build good roads." "They knew how to work together. Look at the neat way the stones are cut and laid." "They believe in safety. See how the wall of stones is built up to prevent going over the edge of the road." She may inquire whether there is any other purpose in extending the retaining wall to form a ledge higher than the roadbed. She certainly will call attention to the fact that this road was built without benefit of modern machinery. The children probably will speculate about the method and equipment actually used in constructing the road before reading to check their hypotheses. Observations which pupils may make are "Look at the bridge over the canyon. I wonder how they managed that!" "They built castles, too." "No, I think it is a fortress." "They made sandals." "That boy is wearing something like our shorts. It must have been warm there." "Sure, the sunshine often makes it hot high up on a mountain." "And the sun is shining. Look at the shadows." "I think he has a serape over his right arm to use at night."

This discussion is typical of any situation where children are accustomed to guided picture interpretation. Typical, too, is the way one child's observation stimulates another's. However, this discussion is not the only method for approaching the topic of Inca civilization. Prior to discussion, the teacher might have given students a few minutes in which to discover five facts about the civilization from the picture. Or, she might have directed children to locate the written text accompanying the picture, read it, study the picture, and then make out questions which they would ask an Inca boy if it were possible to meet him.

The teacher who conducted the picture study from this textbook, *New Ways in the New World*,[3] was fortunate. Most teachers do not have the opportunity to use textbooks which are adequately illustrated. Therefore, it is important that they select from all available sources those pictures which have the greatest value for learning.

---

[3] Todd, Lewis Paul, and Cooper, K. S. *New Ways in the New World.* Morristown, N.J.: Silver Burdett Co., 1954. 350 p.

Over mountain roads the wealth of Peru begins
the long journey to Spain.

A TEXTBOOK ILLUSTRATION SUCH AS THIS CAN BE USED IN SEVERAL
WAYS TO TEACH MANY THINGS ABOUT PERU IN PIZARRO'S TIME. CAN
YOU DISCOVER FIVE FACTS ABOUT THIS CIVILIZATION FROM THE
PICTURE ABOVE? (PHOTO: FROM "NEW WAYS IN THE NEW WORLD,"
BY TODD AND COOPER, SILVER BURDETT CO.)

DISPLAYING PICTURES

If children are studying birds which are typical of their community
—to learn their names and their habits—pictures will be an important
aid to their learning. Some pictures can be shown to the entire class
when the teacher helps them discover distinguishing features of each
bird. These pictures must be large, clear, well lighted, and steadily
supported. Other pictures can be studied by each child alone as he
compares birds and memorizes details. These individual study pictures should be sturdily mounted and accompanied by explicit
captions.

Of the following methods for showing pictures, in groups or individually, the teacher may choose those which best suit her purpose.

Showing Pictures to a Group

A teacher shows pictures to an entire class so that every student
can think about the pictures at the same time she speaks about them.

The purpose: to synchronize the effect of the pictures with her description and interpretation. Group picture viewing is usually the first step in several activities: if the teacher plans a group discussion session in which students will share opinions or compare interpretations or if she plans to establish a mood as a preface to a creative-writing exercise or poetry-listening experience. In either case, the work that follows will be enriched by the initial picture viewing.

Though the easiest way to show a picture to a class is to hold it up in front of the group, this is seldom best. Very few pictures are clear enough in their details or large enough so that the entire class can see them well. But, if a picture suited for group viewing is available, it requires a heavy mount to make it opaque, smooth, and easy to display when held in one hand.

A more efficient procedure for showing a picture—one that needs only simple equipment—is to place it on a stand or easel or in a flash-card holder. The teacher then is free to point out features in the

HOLDING PICTURES WHILE DISCUSSING THEM IN FRONT OF A CLASS IS SELDOM A GOOD IDEA. HERE A STUDENT LEADS THE DISCUSSION WHILE HER TEACHER WATCHES CLOSELY TO SEE IF THE PRESENTATION IS EFFECTIVE FROM A DISTANCE.

THROUGH THE USE OF A FLANNELBOARD, PICTURES CAN LITERALLY
BE CREATED AS A CLASS DISCUSSION DEVELOPS APPROPRIATE CONTENT.
HERE AGAIN, THE PICTURE MATERIAL IS SUPPORTED TO GIVE THE
TEACHER FREEDOM OF MOVEMENT. (PHOTO: FROM THE BAILEY FILM,
"FLANNEL BOARDS AND HOW TO USE THEM")

picture, to gesture while talking, to walk around the room, or to step
to the back of the group to test the picture's effectiveness from a
distance. By this method, a picture can be displayed long enough
for students to discuss it fully and to use it later for reference.

A flannelboard will provide an equally steady support for a picture
and will allow easy, quick changes if a sequence of pictures is being
shown. Additional materials may be arranged for supplementation.
In a lesson about local birds, the title, "Watch for These Birds," could
top the flannelboard and silhouettes of birds could frame the space
for the teaching pictures. Any materials to be placed on a flannelboard
will need patches of flannel, felt, or sandpaper on the back of their
mounts.

A chalkboard also may be used to display pictures. The chalk tray,
of course, can support stiffly mounted pictures. But the chalk tray is
a satisfactory means of display only when children are seated in a
semicircle facing the chalkboard.

A bulletin board of cork or composition is the most generally used piece of equipment for showing pictures. It is permanently placed, usually well lighted, and easy to use. Moreover, students expect to see pictures there; they have picture-reading readiness when they look toward it. A series of pictures can be placed on a bulletin board in planned arrangement. It is easy for the teacher to do the work in advance, and once the series is displayed she can point out to the students the features of each picture, one at a time. But there are disadvantages to this procedure. When a series of pictures is placed close together, it is hard for students to keep their attention synchronized with the teacher's explanation. They may look ahead to other pictures or still be examining a picture already described.

Still another method is for the teacher to pass around, while talking, pictures too small to see from the front of the room. However, this also presents problems. First, the teacher provides competition for herself and for the students. Each person in the group must decide whether to look at the picture or listen to the teacher; it is difficult to do both. Then, by the time the student receives the picture, he may have forgotten what to look for, especially if he listens to the teacher who already is discussing something else. Perhaps the best approach would be for picture viewing to follow explanation. Projected pictures are considerably more effective than simple display methods. Enlargement of picture size removes any doubt whether the boy in the back row can see. But projection brings special problems, too.

In the darkened room the attention of the students can be directed to the picture, but it is easier for the boy in the back seat to daydream, or, unable to see the teacher, he may find it hard to keep track of what she is saying. Group discussion of the picture, too, is sometimes less successful in darkened quarters.

The brilliant picture in the darkened room can heighten an emotional mood the teacher may be trying to create. But the special efforts involved in darkening the room and in focusing the projector may break the mood of a lesson. Even if the mechanical details are adjusted before the lesson, a break in continuity and mood is almost inevitable when projected pictures are interspersed through a talk.

The advantages and problems of a darkened room are especially true for the opaque projector, but its usefulness hardly can be denied. With this projector, pictures in books, magazines, and newspapers or maps, drawings, and photographs—in fact, any fairly flat article up to 10″ x 10″—can be reproduced and enlarged on the screen. In

USING AN OPAQUE PROJECTOR. THIS DRAMATICS CLASS IS ABLE TO CONCENTRATE ATTENTION ON AUTHENTIC PICTURES OF THE MANNERS AND CUSTOMS, DRESS AND LOCALE OF THE PERIOD THEY ARE TO PORTRAY IN THEIR NEXT PRODUCTION. (PHOTO: UNIVERSITY SCHOOL, OHIO STATE UNIVERSITY)

addition, the equipment is easy to use and subject to few mechanical failures.

Showing Pictures to Individuals

When a student looks at pictures by himself, he wants time to study and a place where it will be reasonably quiet and comfortable. Maybe he will copy or trace the picture. Perhaps he will compare it carefully with other pictures. Whatever he will do, the teacher should provide him with a quiet corner, good light, and well-mounted, captioned pictures.

Pictures for individual study, suitably captioned and titled, may be anchored to a bulletin board, pegboard, or clothesline. But since concentration is better achieved at a quiet desk location, only those pictures that make their point on fairly quick examination or that can be easily seen from the student's desk should be so displayed.

Projected and enlarged pictures are well suited for individual viewing, although one tends to think of them as practical only

PICTURES APPROACH REALITY
AS THIS FIRST-GRADE CHILD
STUDIES AND COMPARES.
NOTE THAT HER "RESEARCH"
HAS BEEN HELPFULLY
SIMPLIFIED BY RUBBER BANDS
ON THE BOOK.
AN IMAGINATIVE TEACHER MAY
LATER USE AN OPAQUE PROJECTOR
TO SHARE THIS PROJECT
WITH THE CLASS.
(PHOTO: CARL PURCELL, NEA)

for group showing. The enlarged picture, the focused attention, and the dramatic effect help the student when he is studying alone. A small folding screen can be set up so that it forms its own pocket of darkness in a regularly lighted room, and one student can use the area for looking at slides or filmstrips. Slides may be viewed in an enlarger, which has its own strong light source. The stereoscope makes possible the individual viewing of three-dimensional pictures, though special picture sets must be purchased along with it. Old news pictures can be studied through use of the microfilm projector. (The expanding use of microfilm promises to provide much picture material via this medium.)

A well-selected picture is an effective teaching aid only if it is carefully shown to the students. Whether they see it alone or with the rest of their class, whether they see it projected or flat, they can get its full value only if its presentation is planned carefully and thoughtfully.

Practical Aids to Display

Lack of proper respect for materials is the only explanation for the obvious abuse to pictures in many displays. Picture materials should not be anchored to walls, chalkboards, or bulletin boards by means of tape or thumbtacks driven through the picture or mount.

On page 36 is a reproduction of a sheet which is distributed to prospective teachers by the Teaching Aids Laboratory of The Ohio State University.

Figure 1B shows how Dennison Cloth Suspension Rings No. 21 provide adequate space for insertion of thumbtacks. These rings also provide means for hanging flat picture materials on hooks or nails.

Figure 1C shows use of metal eyelets. These eyelets can be inserted into paper or cardboard material quickly and permanently by means of a small hand-operated eyeleter, a device sold in notions departments or by dealers in leather supplies. When eyelets are used in paper, it is wise to reinforce the top of the paper on the reverse side with an inch-wide strip of tape, preferably gummed cloth mending tape. This reinforcement provides strength and thickness for holding fast the inserted eyelets. When eyelets are uniformly spaced in all of the school's chart-size material, filing and display are simplified. Metal grommets, available in several sizes and inserted with a special punch, are recommended for very heavy materials. Grommets and eyelets can be purchased from most office-supply firms. Both fit over hooks found on classroom display rails.

Because relatively few classrooms are equipped for proper display of materials, teachers frequently improvise their own devices. Display hangers for hanging maps and charts from any molding are good commercially produced devices. If they are not found locally, they can be ordered from map-supply houses. Schools not equipped with any classroom display devices may wish to investigate display rails and accessories also sold by leading map-supply houses.

Easels purchased ready made or constructed in the school shop also are used for displaying mounted pictures. Some easels are equipped with display hooks; others are constructed with crossbars between which the top of the chart is placed. Screws and nuts used at the ends of the bars make it possible to hold the chart in place.

EIGHT WAYS TO DISPLAY PICTURES*

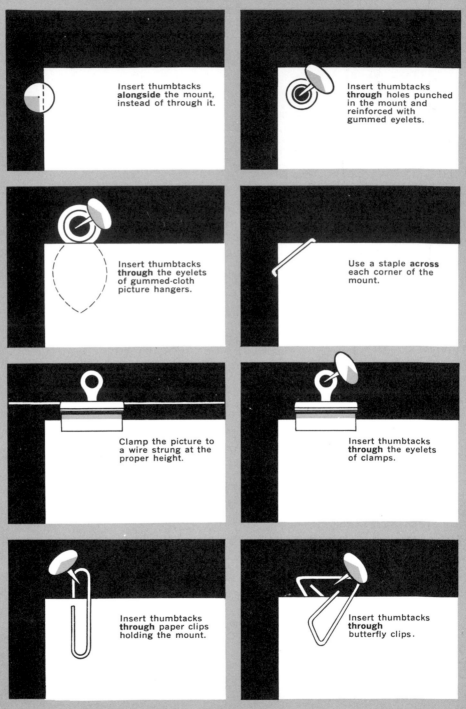

Insert thumbtacks **alongside** the mount, instead of through it.

Insert thumbtacks **through** holes punched in the mount and reinforced with gummed eyelets.

Insert thumbtacks **through** the eyelets of gummed-cloth picture hangers.

Use a staple **across** each corner of the mount.

Clamp the picture to a wire strung at the proper height.

Insert thumbtacks **through** the eyelets of clamps.

Insert thumbtacks **through** paper clips holding the mount.

Insert thumbtacks **through** butterfly clips.

---

* Dale, Edgar. *Audio-Visual Methods in Teaching.* Revised edition. New York: Dryden Press, 1954. p. 257.

An inexpensive desk easel may be made from plywood or heavy cardboard.

In place of easels or bulletin boards, some teachers keep a large sheet of boxboard or Upson Board in their classrooms. This sheet, placed on the chalkboard tray, provides a display surface similar to a bulletin board. Charts may be anchored to sheets, just as to bulletin boards, by means of staples (Figure 1D) inserted with a staple gun. Large charts may be anchored by means of clamps on wire (Figure 1E) or very large paper clips fastened over the top of chart and board (Figure 1F).

Another material which makes an excellent display board, either permanent or portable, is pegboard. Available at many hardware stores, it can be cut to any size and offers multiple possibilities for combining display of both flat and three-dimensional materials.

PROCESSING PICTURES

Processing pictures includes all steps necessary to prepare picture materials for filing and use. Most commercially sold picture materials are printed on heavy stock and usually are adequately captioned. Pictures, clippings from books, magazines, and other sources have to be mounted, and captions and labels have to be supplied. If, at the time these pictures are cut out, the caption is lightly written on the back and copied off when mounted, there will be no doubt about the picture's identity.

Protective Covering for Pictures

All flat picture materials are handled frequently and, when in use, are exposed to classroom dust. Therefore, for extended use, they should be treated with a protective coating. Plastic spray coatings which are sold at bookshops for use on picture materials work quite well, but under some conditions tend to chip and flake off.

Self-sticking sheet-plastic coatings are available in both a clear-shiny and dull-matte finish. At present such coating is expensive both because of the cost of the material and because of the time involved in cutting it to size and applying it. However, for expensive or rare items in the collection, it is economical since it prolongs the life of the material indefinitely. This plastic can be ordered (under the name of Permafilm) from Denoyer-Geppert Company, 5235-5239 Ravenswood Avenue, Chicago 40, Illinois.

Another protective covering available is the envelope type, wherein the picture slides between two sheets of transparent plastic. This type of covering provides excellent protection, but in most situations is prohibitively expensive for all but very special items in the collection. Plastic sheet laminations are stocked by most library supply firms and by many bookstores. A word of caution is in order here. Some of the clear plastic surfaces reflect light and thereby produce a glare unsatisfactory for picture viewing.

Mounting Picture Materials

A picture is mounted to set it off well, to provide ease in handling and filing, and to prolong its usefulness. The mounting of pictures can be a work of art. Any picture can be set off to advantage by careful selection of type, size, color, and texture of mount. In the small classroom collection, such consideration can be given to each picture. If the collection is large, such consideration of each picture is impractical and must be reserved for expensive works of art or other rare pictures.

Many museums and libraries use a standard white or off-white mounting board for flat picture material. This board is rigid, durable, and available in standard sizes. However, it is somewhat expensive, it soils, and it yellows with age. For less expensive, serviceable mounts in the 9" x 12" and 12" x 18" size, a cover paper (the weight used to cover small pamphlets) or Lines Pulpwood No. 80 are both satisfactory. The cover paper is available from most paper manufacturing companies; the Lines Pulpwood No. 80 is handled by most library supply dealers. The cover paper takes up little space in files and is not too expensive for replacement when the mount becomes too soiled or worn for attractive display.

The Mount. The choice of color is an important consideration. Since the function of the mount is to set off the picture well, the color of the mount should bring out those in the picture; it must never compete with them. Unless each picture can be given such special attention that a minor color in it can be picked up for the mount, neutral colors are most satisfactory. Cover paper in warm tones of gray or tan furnishes a pleasing background, and one or the other of these colors harmonizes with those of most colored pictures.

For large chart-type materials which obviously need to be mounted, Chipboard No. 4 provides an inexpensive and satisfactorily rigid material. There is no choice of color; it is available only in gray.

Adherents for Mounting. Rubber cement, sold for use with paper, is an easy-to-use and a universally available adhesive. When purchased by the gallon, along with rubber cement thinner, the overall cost is reduced appreciably. To make a temporary mounting, the rubber cement is applied to the back of the picture only, and allowed to become tacky before it is placed in position on the mount. To make a permanent mounting, the rubber cement is applied to each surface —the back of the picture and the mount—and then allowed to become tacky before the picture is placed in position on the mount.

Another mounting process is dry mounting, for which a special dry mounting tissue is required. With this tissue, an iron, and a little practice, anyone can master the process. It is shown step by step in the filmstrip, *Mounting Pictures.*[4] This filmstrip is the best single source available on the subject of picture mounting.

For very large charts, the wet mounting process is often used. This process is shown step by step in the film, *Wet Mounting Pictorial Materials,*[5] available from Indiana University for loan or purchase.

Simplified written directions for the wet mounting process on cloth follow.

Materials:

A fairly large, smooth-surfaced table, any good floor wax, cloth for applying wax, wheat-base wallpaper paste powder, a container for holding paste mixture, a tongue depressor or other tool for mixing. When a number of maps are to be mounted, expense is less if unbleached muslin is purchased by the bolt. Also time is saved if several maps are mounted successively at one session.

Preparation:

1. Wax the table surface that is to be used for mounting process.
2. Mix desired amount of paste (see directions on container). Mix with water to consistency of maple syrup.
3. Cut to size a piece of unbleached muslin, allowing an additional three inches in all directions.

---

[4] *Mounting Pictures.* 52 frames, color. University of Texas, Visual Instruction Bureau, Austin 12, Texas, 1956.

[5] *Wet Mounting Pictorial Materials.* 11 min., 16 mm, sound, color and b & w. Indiana University, Audio-Visual Center, Bloomington, Indiana, 1952.

4. Tack or staple cloth tightly (do not stretch) over waxed table top.
5. If a map is quite valuable, you may wish to run a water-fastness test by thoroughly wetting a small portion of it to make certain that the color is fast and the paper tough enough to handle when wet.

Mounting:
1. Wet thoroughly both cloth and map.
2. Brush paste on entire surface and work well into the cloth.
3. Brush paste on entire surface of reverse side of map.
4. Place map on cloth; smooth lightly with fingers.
5. Let map alone until paste is tacky enough for bubbles to disappear, permitting map to remain flat when pressed.
6. Press map flat with roller, repeating the rolling process until the map is perfectly flat.
7. Allow the map to dry naturally; use no artificial heat. Drying will take at least 12 hours.
8. Remove tacks from cloth. Then remove map from table with one rapid upward pull.
9. Trim edges, leaving enough cloth at the top to staple into a window shade roller, or enough at both top and bottom to insert into wooden half-rounds.[6]

Unique Problems. Some flat picture materials that can be suitably mounted on either 9" x 12" or 12" x 18" mounts present unique problems. For example, an excellent study print often has a valuable explanation printed on the reverse side. Frequently both sides of a pictorial page in a periodical are equally valuable. Often no duplicates are obtainable. In instances such as these, either of two methods of mounting may be employed to make possible access to both sides of the page. First is the simple and popular method of placing the top of the picture flush with the top of the mount and anchoring it with hinges. Since the rest of the sheet is left free, it will flip over to expose the reverse side of the picture on the reverse side of the mount. Another method involves the use of two sheets of mounting paper, each cut out to form frames. Edges of the picture can be anchored between the frames and the frames held fast with adhesive.

---

[6] See *A Guide for Use with the Indiana University Film Series in the Area of Preparation and Use of Audio-Visual Instructional Materials.* Bloomington: Audio-Visual Center, Indiana University, 1958. 107 p.

From periodicals such as *Holiday* or *Life*, the teacher often wants to mount a double page. Hinged, the double spread is difficult to file and tears readily; opened out, it is outsized for filing. Very often it is possible to mount each page on a separate sheet, but arranged on the sheet so as to fit together perfectly when displayed. Double-page mounts should bear some code label (perhaps a particular style or color signal dot or label placed on each half) so that each half can be readily identified as requiring its companion part.

Post cards and other small pictures are valuable for individual study and for use in the opaque projector. For use in an opaque projector, small pictures should be placed uniformly on mounts large enough to insure proper placement during projection.

Clippings also present problems of mounting and filing. The small single-page clipping can be fastened to a mount, as is a picture. The longer clipping is satisfactorily handled by stapling it into a standard filing folder.

Filing Picture Materials. To enable teacher and students alike to locate a picture when it is needed, every classroom should be equipped with a well-organized file. In many schools a letter-size file of steel or wood is standard classroom equipment. The legal-size file is preferable, for it will accommodate 10" x 14" photographs and prints. In the vast number of schools where files are not furnished, imaginative teachers have adapted other containers, such as heavy cardboard cartons and orange crates, to serve the purpose. A coat of enamel of the same color as the classroom wall gives the improvised file a finished look and at the same time provides a wipe-clean surface.

In building collections, the oversized, or 12" x 18," mounts are sometimes filed in wooden bins which have been specially constructed to accommodate a vertical file of mounts. Mounts of this size can also be filed in deep cupboards equipped with dividers or pigeonholes similar to those in record cabinets. In fact, record cabinets are sometimes adapted for the purpose. When the index information is placed at the bottom outer edge of legal-size folders and alphabetical indexing is indicated on the shelf itself, material is easily located. When cupboards cannot be built by industrial arts departments, deep cupboards may be adapted by placing dividers fashioned from heavy cardboard between the folders on the shelves. With brush pen, index information can be placed on index tabs (index tabs can be purchased in 12-inch strips and cut to desired size) which in turn are placed on the dividers. When there are not a great many pictures to be stored, cardboard dividers can be used horizontally on closely spaced shelving at eye level or lower. Bold lettering with brush pen on large index tabs facilitates location of materials.

While the files thus far discussed accommodate most of the illustrations, paintings, sketches, photographs, prints of various sorts, and cartoons, they will not take care of the charts, graphs, posters, and post cards which the teacher may have collected. Metal or cardboard card files or shoe boxes adapted for the purpose make satisfactory files for post cards.

Unless mounted on half-rounds of dowel, chart-type materials should lie flat while stored, to prevent buckle and curl when hung. Many modern classrooms are equipped with built-in features especially designed for storing poster-size materials. On the other hand, teachers must furnish their own storage files in a number of situations. Protective covering for chart materials may be fashioned from two pieces of Upson Board cut to size and hinged either with linen tape or strips of unbleached muslin. The muslin can be fastened to the

AN INCREASING AMOUNT OF USEFUL PICTURE MATERIAL PRESENTS UNIQUE STORAGE AND RETRIEVAL PROBLEMS IN NEARLY EVERY CLASS-ROOM, AND NEW SCHOOLS MUST BE PLANNED TO ACCOMMODATE THIS DEVELOPMENT. (PHOTO: CALIFORNIA STATE DEPARTMENT OF EDUCA-TION)

board with either LePage's or Weldwood glue. The glue should be applied to the board and permitted to become tacky before the muslin is put in place. Use of a rubber roller or rolling pin will smooth out wrinkles in the cloth. After 12 hours the glue should be dry and the hard-back folder ready for use. These folders prove somewhat more sturdy than do the oversized envelopes which some teachers fashion from wrapping paper. If some sort of fastener is added, these folders may be placed upright to slide behind a desk, table, or other portable piece of furniture.

In some classrooms teachers have installed their own personally designed chart racks. One such rack designed to hold in upright positions several of the "envelopes" made from wrapping paper was a simple but sturdy structure with bottom and ends made from solid wood and sides fashioned from strips of wood evenly spaced and anchored to the end pieces.

In the larger collections, such as an entire building collection, the 9" x 12" size mounts are easily filed in ordinary filing cabinets in regular manila filing folders, preferably with titles typed in capital letters on colored labels selected to provide contrast. An adequate system of cross referencing makes for maximum efficiency in utilization of the collection. In place of standard cross-reference sheets which have no rigidity, use of half (this gives a single sheet) of a standard filing folder provides inexpensive, easy-to-handle cross-reference sheets. When these sheets uniformly bear labels which contrast with the labels used on the regular filing folders, they are readily identified as further aids to location of desired materials.

Filing Chart-Type Materials in Building Collections. Because charts, maps, and posters are variously mounted, filing of these materials must be worked out for each type of mounting. Some of these materials are of heavy-duty stock which requires no mounting. To prolong the life of unmounted materials, they should be filed face down, and the label on the reverse side of each piece should carry sufficient data to reduce handling to a minimum. Overhandling in locating and refiling such materials often causes more wear than does use. A vast number of charts and maps can be filed in a single map case. Charts stacked face down, one on top of the other, should be consecutively numbered. Any item can be readily located and slipped out from the stack, if labels are uniformly placed on the reverse side of each item at the corner most easily read when any drawer of the case is opened. If these labels bear the drawer number, the catalog number, and the title written large with brush pen, refiling as well as locating is simplified.

Plan of Organization. A simple alphabetical organization is ordinarily most useful, especially when a complete card index is not feasible. However, classroom files should be organized according to whatever plan is most functional in the particular situation. Many teachers report that organization by teaching units is more satisfactory than by subject. This means that in primary classrooms, under the heading *Animals,* subheads might be *Circus Animals, Farm Animals, Pets,* and *Small Animals of the Woods,* because teaching units are so organized.

That the classification system be consistent with the maturity level of the students is of major concern to every teacher who understands how to use pictures effectively as resources for learning. Also, it is important that headings, subheadings, and cross references be geared to the reading level of the boys and girls. For labeling dividers, teachers might well investigate the write-on, self-adhering plastic tapes available at office-supply stores. Some of these tapes have margins in color; for example, black margins may be used to indicate major headings, and another color may be used to indicate subheads.

A few words about the essential information that should be placed *on the reverse side* of each picture mount. For identification purposes, the name of the school or other owner should be affixed with a rubber stamp. A rubber stamp, made to order for a nominal fee, saves time otherwise involved in manual writing. To facilitate refiling of materials, information such as *Transportation—Air—Jet Propulsion I* is helpful. This indicates that the picture belongs in the folder marked *Jet Propulsion I* under *Transportation,* section *Air.* This information should be placed in the upper left-hand corner, the point on which the eye habitually focuses first for reading.

Establishing a Simple Plan of Distribution of Picture Materials in Building Situations. Picture materials should be located in a place accessible to both teachers and students at all times. For this reason, places such as the principal's office are not a desirable storage center for even small collections. Location is but one of the major considerations in making materials readily available. If there is no school librarian or teacher assigned to take over the responsibilities, either the school or the public library staff might be asked to assist in setting up a simple charging and record system.

A simplified system which has functioned satisfactorily in some buildings operates on somewhat the following pattern. In place of a catalog, a listing of all resource materials contained in the collection is placed for ready reference in the first drawer of the first filing cabinet. The dictionary type of alphabetical arrangement is used for the files, hence this same plan augmented by cross references is used for the listing. On the listing, the location of items is noted, for example, *Cupboard 4–Shelf 1*, for items not contained in the vertical files. Duplicate copies of this listing are furnished to all teachers. A card index transfer file for 3″ x 5″ cards placed on top of the first filing cabinet serves as a simple charge file.

Any faculty committee can complete plans for charge data which may be mimeographed on 3″ x 5″ cards. A box adequate to hold a number of blank charge cards and pencils conveniently anchored beside the charge file saves steps and makes it easy for the teacher or student drawing out material to fill out a card and file the charge card *alphabetically by title of material withdrawn*. This plan of charging makes it possible for other teachers desiring the same item to contact the borrower and work out arrangements for sharing limited resources.

When the building staff is willing and anxious to work out cooperatively a plan adapted to their needs and resources, any school, anywhere, can have a growing picture collection.

SIX PICTURES, SIX POINTS OF VIEW OF ONE SUBJECT, PRESENT THE STUDENT WITH A CLEAR IDEA OF THE SETTING AND STATURE OF THE UNITED NATIONS. (PHOTOS: UNITED NATIONS)

Pictures for Subject-Matter Areas

In the preceding chapters discussion has been on general recommendations for choosing pictures—why they are valuable in teaching and what makes them so—and methods for using pictures—how to display them and help children learn from them. This chapter is more specific in approach. It contains descriptions of situations in which teachers have found pictures helpful for learning in various subjects taught in the schools. Though the descriptions are divided by subject matter, since no area of learning exists unrelated to another area of learning, some interweaving of material will be found. For example, pictures for building mathematical concepts are described primarily in the section on *Arithmetic and Mathematics*, but also are discussed in the sections on *Business Education, Homemaking*, and *Social Studies*. A good procedure for the teacher interested in one special subject would be to read the entire chapter before centering attention on the section most pertinent to that subject.

ARITHMETIC AND MATHEMATICS

In the discussion which follows, attempt is made to indicate some of the ways pictures can be used to aid the understanding of arithmetic and mathematics. It is hoped that these illustrations will suggest to teachers numerous other ways in which pictures can contribute to this area of learning.

Number Concepts

In the early primary grades pictures furnish representations of objects for developing number concepts. For example, pictures of three dolls, three bicycles, or the like serve to establish "threeness" and to build recognition of a group. A picture of three boys and two pairs of cowboy boots provides material for the question, "Do we need

more pairs of boots and, if so, how many?" For this work, some teachers display the pictures on feltboard; others mount their cutouts on large sheets of durable paper.

To handle number situations, young children must master a new vocabulary, and pictures play a part. For example, such simple materials as cutouts of five automobiles, different in color and size, can be used on feltboard to build vocabulary. The following are problems to accompany the exhibit:

1. Which cars are *longer than* the yellow one?
2. Arrange the cars in a row and put the *longest* car *first*.
3. Make *two* rows of cars. Put *two* cars in the *first* row. How many are there in the *second* row?
4. Which is the *shortest* car in the *second* row?

The collecting and organizing of pictures by a class helps to clarify number concepts. A third-grade group brought in pictures of items sold in pairs. When they began to organize their pictures, they discovered two categories, a pair of two separate items and a pair of two identical parts attached to form a single item.

When the teacher shows interest in helping children discover what a new word, *triangle,* has in common with tricycle and triplet, she may find that the class is interested in starting a collection of pictures, "Name Words That Contain Number Hints." Pictures of a quartet and of the Pentagon building started one such collection.

Word Origins

To explain the origin of the word *calculate,* the teacher shows a picture as she tells the class the word comes from calculus, a little calx or limestones used as counting stones, a crude forerunner of the modern adding machine. Then, having seen illustrations of a few sample words, students need little encouragement to create their own illustrations for other new words they are taught.

More mature students are interested in stories behind such words as bank, broker, budget, calculate, cancel, coin, salary, record, and tally. Stories of these words, some of which are illustrated, are found in *Picturesque Word Origins.*[1]

Illustrations of word origins are good material for a mathematics bulletin board, "Did *You* Know?" Mathematics teachers miss opportunities to develop appreciative insight if they do not have a special bulletin board where students, with the teacher's help, display cartoons, original sketches, or clipped pictures which underscore mathematical concepts.

The Principle of Measurement

Tables are often constructed to explain measurement. Following plans for making butter, a second-grade class and teacher together constructed a pictorial measurement table ("Measures We Need To Know"). In the later grades, when more complete tables of weights and measures are essential, collecting pictures of items sold by the liquid quart and the dozen broadens understanding.

When children learn to read parts of an inch on the ruler or compare United States linear measurements with metric equivalents, magnifications of a section of the ruler and a section of the meter stick are helpful. These magnifications also aid in teaching addition and subtraction of fractional and decimal parts and in making comparison of fractional and decimal equivalents.

For teaching meter reading—thermometers, speedometers, gas or electric meters—pictures of their dials or scales large enough to read are introduced, so that computation takes on practical value.

---

[1] *Picturesque Word Origins.* Springfield, Mass.: G. C. Merriam Co., 1933. 144 p.

Measurement becomes an interesting topic for students when they work together to collect and arrange items for an exhibit of instruments of measurement. Measurement becomes a meaningful topic when students realize something of the origin of measuring instruments and of the role measurement has played in man's struggle to gain control of his environment. A well-illustrated book makes the origin of standard measures a story of man's ingenuity. Selected pictures from such a book, used in the opaque projector, provide valuable material.

Buying and Selling

Full-page pictorial advertisements from catalogs or daily papers provide an up-to-the-minute setting for exercises on buying and selling. Young children can play store with these pictures. By placing price tags on the items in the "picture" store, they gain experience in reading and writing amounts of money. More mature students may find special advertisements for exercises with the directions, "What items can you buy for under a dollar and how much change will you receive?" Advertisements for special sales—"One-Fourth Off Sale" or "Storewide, 10% Off"—are also useful for discussion or for written exercises.

Pictures are used to explain costs which, taken together, determine the retail price of an item. A bulletin board is used to work out the cost story of a simple article, such as a sweater. Pictures would include a picture of a farmer with his sheep, a freight car transporting wool to the mill, and—finally—the sweater in a retail store.

For the study of buying and selling, a teacher introduces the terms first cost, margin, overhead, profit, and selling price, which are more meaningful if accompanied by a diagram and pictures. A diagram showing the relationships between these terms may fill an entire bulletin board.

The Business of Banking

Students should be helped to learn how to do business with a bank. The best method is a school study trip. Following the trip, the teacher may extend and reinforce learning through pictures showing the layout and routine in banks larger than the one visited. As a means of summarizing this information, the class arranges a series of pictures to show the services banks perform or the steps involved in opening a savings account.

In some schools, children are given the opportunity of setting up . their own bank; picture study of small banks introduces the project. As additional experience, teachers arrange for children's checks to be negotiable at neighborhood stores.

Insurance and Taxes

Topics of social significance, such as insurance and taxes, should be taught so that students are informed of social implications as well as arithmetical concepts. Students who collect pictures of the items on which there is a luxury tax will note what are considered luxuries by our lawmakers. As prospective voters, they can appraise these items and judge which are obviously luxuries and which seem to be essentials. When the study of taxes is introduced, students gain insight into the need for them on the federal, state, and local levels if they arrange a series of bulletin boards to illustrate the benefits derived from federal, state, and local governments.

Mathematics for Everyday Life

Mathematics should be taught so that children experience its usefulness in interpreting statements in books and pictures. When inland children study Europe and see a picture of the "Queen Mary" as a ship on which to make a trip, the teacher gives them an idea of its size by making comparison with the familiar, "How does the ship's length compare with a city block or with the tallest building in our town?" Pictures of the swimming pool on the "Queen Mary" or of her first-class dining room are compared in size with the school gymnasium, the cafeteria, or the auditorium. Through this approach, students develop the insight and the disposition to use mathematics for broadening the base of their understanding.

The imaginative teacher often uses pictures to lend drama and significance to life-related situations, especially where first-hand experiences known to the students would cause embarrassment. In a school community where an excessive amount of credit buying is common, a teacher made extensive use of pictures for study of the practice. In preparation, she obtained permission from two local stores to photograph the items recovered during a one-week period because purchasers had not met payments. Most of the items photographed fell into the luxury class. A study of the pictures pointed up the large amount of money irrevocably lost to consumers through installment buying and raised the important question of what the consumer should know to protect his interests.

An advertisement of a couple enjoying a high-fidelity recording with the text, "This pleasure can be yours for as little as $1 down and $1 a week," was shown by opaque projection. Guided discussion led students to raise the questions: "For how many weeks?" "What part of the payment is carrying charge?" "What is the total cost under this plan?" "What is the total cost if payment is made on a cash-sale basis?" Later, several pictures were used as case studies to develop insight into the values which make installment buying intelligent in one case, extravagant in another, and alarmingly shortsighted in yet another.

Higher Mathematics

Pictures are an aid in the study of geometric shapes. When young children are learning to identify common shapes—circle, square, rectangle, and triangle—they can collect pictures of objects to be mounted on charts or displayed on bulletin boards with the title, "These Are Rectangular Shapes." As children mature these activities increase in complexity. Students of plane geometry collect pictures for a bulletin board, "Geometry in Art," on which they display pictures of stained-glass windows, Indian blankets, pottery, and architecture. On an-

THIS DISCUSSION OF A BASIC MATHEMATICAL STRUCTURE—A GROUP OF SIX ELEMENTS—IS CENTERED ON PICTURES OF GEOMETRIC SHAPES IN SEVERAL COLORS. (PHOTO: CARL PURCELL, NEA)

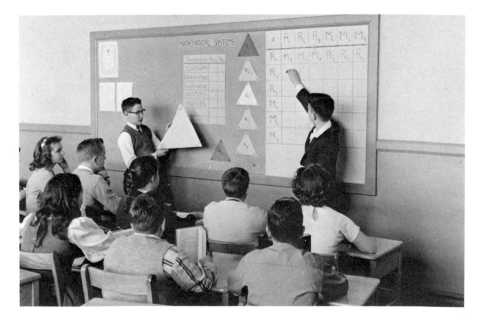

other occasion, the bulletin board is mounted to show that plane geometric figures can be identified in forms around us: a lamp post, a gate, a college pennant, a road sign. The teacher may use pictures to demonstrate the five fundamental loci, and to show how loci are involved in our everyday living—the planning of a railroad or the charting of the course of an aircraft. Pictures of containers collected from advertisements are used—cans (cylinders) or boxes (cubes)— to round out a collection on industrial uses of solid geometric figures.

To older students, the study of the more abstract aspects of the mathematics program—algebra and geometry—often is presented so that they are unenthusiastic about taking the courses. For this reason, students readily forget the content and, what is still worse, they fail to develop the skill of thinking critically. When geometry is taught to illustrate the meaning of proof, working out theorems becomes a meaningful guide to all critical thinking. With this approach, students of geometry work not only with mathematical experiences pertaining directly to geometry but also with nonmathematical experiences. For nonmathematical experiences, advertisements and cartoons are used as study material. In advertisements, pictures and words are analyzed to determine what assumptions are implied through the picture, what logical implication can be made, and what terms need to be defined. After the merits have been discussed in the study of proof (both direct and indirect), members of the class collect advertisements which illustrate and clarify each type of proof. The advertisements also make students alert to the danger of being carried along to unwarranted conclusions.

BUSINESS EDUCATION

In a high school where tiresome drills and uninspiring exercises had characterized the curriculum, a teacher of business education was asked to put new life into the program. Pictures helped the teacher fulfill this assignment.

Office Practice

First step was the department bulletin board. On it, the teacher displayed enlargements of cartoons selected from his file of pictures on office practice. Cartoons were enlarged with the aid of the opaque projector, and the projected outlines were traced on poster paper. Ball-point pen and India ink were used to finish the tracings as simple line drawings, with occasional use of art pencils for touches of color.

Changed frequently, the bulletin boards soon became a center of interest for the entire student body. Before long, students of business education took over responsibility for them, and even developed original cartoons for display.

A classroom bulletin board also was begun. Sometimes a question pertinent to the day's discussion—"What Do You Have To Give the Job?"—was posted. Under this question, captioned illustrations represented poise, good work habits, and other key qualities. Occasionally arranged in sequential order, as in "Hired-Tired-Fired," the board was used as the target for one point in a day's lesson.

Office Machines

For teaching the operation of a business machine, large charts, diagrams, and pictures showing the process step-by-step were used along with a visual demonstration. Following the demonstration, students and teacher worked out concise and helpful legends for the pictorial aids selected for display above the machines. Pictures without any legends or markings were sometimes used for oral review and for testing correct machine operations. Pictures of machines not owned by the school were studied so that, when taken on field trips to local business firms, students would understand key features of these machines and be able to follow explanations of their operation.

At times, pictures played a role in assignments. To give interesting, purposeful practice in preparing copy and using the spirit duplicator, a teacher assigned committee projects. Each committee was made responsible for working up ditto copies to demonstrate the variety of copy possible for reproduction. Copy in each case was prepared to announce, advertise, or explain a coming event—a school affair, a class or club project, a PTA meeting, or some local event of interest to the student body. Original sketches made with colors of ditto carbon were encouraged. From among prepared copies, those judged by the class as best were displayed on an all-school bulletin board.

Organization for Work

Close-up photos of desks and desk drawers were compared so that students could make their own judgments about efficient methods of organization. Organization of files and systems of labeling were also studied and compared by means of pictures. Illustrations were enlarged in the opaque projector to a size convenient for detailed study. This projector was also used to show samples of business forms. Later, the teacher made permanent wall-size business forms on window shades previously coated with chalkboard paint. These pictures could be displayed before the class to speed up the process of learning to use the forms.

Typing Skills

When students in a beginning typing class were sufficiently experienced to appreciate the strain and fatigue caused by faulty posture at the typewriter, the teacher supplemented the textbook illustration on postural habits with pictures of the bone and muscle framework and pictures of correct and faulty posture at the typewriter. By contrast and comparison, the students understood the teacher's insistence on correct posture. Following this display, each member of the class made an original poster on posture. Typical poster titles were "Don't Be a Droop," "Bodies Object, Sit Erect," and "Let's Train So Muscles Won't Complain."

Pictures of typewriting techniques were introduced when students learned the keyboard and had enough experience to welcome and appreciate the use of timesavers and other procedures for keeping copy neat and eliminating extra motion. Students' basic typing experience helped them to analyze critically pictures used to present new techniques.

EXPERIENCED TYPISTS
AND BEGINNERS WILL SEE
IN PICTURES SUCH AS THIS
MANY MATTERS TO DISCUSS.
SUCH PICTURES
ALSO PROVE USEFUL
WITH STUDENT TEACHERS.
(PHOTO: CARL PURCELL, NEA)

Practical Work Experience

Arrangements were made with local factories, shops, and stores for all members of a class (two students to each place of business) to spend a half day as visiting aides to familiarize themselves with the working of an office. To share their visiting experiences with one another, students made use of mounted pictures and photographs selected from the section of the picture files devoted to on-the-job duties.

Arrangements also were made with the school office for students to take turns acting as receptionist-typists and typists for the school faculty. This work gave them first-hand experience and an immediate reason for the study of good grooming, office dress, office etiquette, and telephone manners. Here again, illustrations, photographs, and cartoons were used to demonstrate some of the *do's* and *don't's* of working in an office and to stress important business practices.

While working in the school office, students were confronted with problems of getting along with others. Pictures which demonstrated general problems in human relations—with possible office application —furnished the basis for classroom discussion to clarify what is considered good manners on the job.

FOREIGN LANGUAGES

When a class entered the room where they were to begin their study of Spanish, they found pictures bearing captions in Spanish and some objects from Latin America labeled in Spanish. Students were attracted to the exhibits and found the captions and labels a challenge as they tried to establish a relationship between picture or object and its caption. Once the school term was under way, students gladly cooperated with the teacher to make the room pleasant for learning by creating similar displays.

Vocabulary Building

The teacher of any foreign language finds that, for vocabulary building, use of flat pictures to identify objects and activities adds interest, saves time, and greatly reduces classroom use of English. Usually, learning is accelerated and forgetting minimized when the auditory and visual symbols are presented simultaneously.

Pictures can be used to enliven oral and written practice in the study of a foreign language. Selection of pictures for this purpose should be governed by the target for the lesson and the age and interests of the learners. Color usually adds interest but is not an essential element. The activities of persons in the picture, however, must be familiar and clearly shown; for example, a picture of a postman delivering mail to a home where the housewife and her young son are eagerly awaiting him. This picture could be used as the basis for a conversation written on a reading chart by the teacher. Students would refer to the picture for cues in interpreting the written symbols. The picture could also be used to suggest the content for a role playing exercise in which students would take the parts of the characters in the picture.

By pointing up need for specific vocabulary, pictures aid in the introduction of a lesson. In a lesson on numbers, for example, the teacher might select a picture of a Mexican railway station or a Brazilian airport, a place where how much, how many, and how long all would be pertinent. Suppose the teacher selects a picture of a man at a ticket window in a railway station. If the students imagine themselves in his place, they would consider what questions he might ask. They would be ready to learn the new words which would enable them to frame appropriate questions.

NEW TECHNIQUES IN TEACHING
FOREIGN LANGUAGES
HAVE INCREASED THE USE
OF PICTURE MATERIAL
IN THIS GROWING AND IMPORTANT
CURRICULUM AREA.
(PHOTO: CARL PURCELL, NEA)

Culture Patterns

For work with beginners and advanced students of foreign language, pictures are aids to learning about the culture patterns in the areas of the language under study. Such pictures encourage discussion of the similarities and differences between the cultural pattern of the students' native country and that of the area where the foreign language is spoken.

When elementary-school children study a foreign language—French, for example—they identify with the French culture by playing games and singing songs of French children. Pictures illustrate how these activities are carried on in France. In some schools—elementary and secondary—students exchange correspondence, pictures, and tape recordings with foreign students. In one school, a group of tenth graders projected pictures sent by their German correspondents.

The opaque projector is a boon to the language teacher; it makes possible group study of colored post cards printed in foreign lands, color plates from books on other parts of the world, and any materials which are otherwise too small to be effective for class use.

Students cannot grasp the feelings and thoughts of another people only by using the words of that culture; they must share in the lives of the people, know their customs, their music, their literature. Dramatizing the life and activities of a people builds understanding. And pictures are invaluable as aids to students in making scenery, stage properties, and costumes authentic. Sometimes, when a specific backdrop is needed, a picture is projected directly onto stage flats and traced in preparation for painting.

Classes in English

Americanization classes and any other classes where English is taught to those unfamiliar with the language are foreign language classes also. Here, the problem is not only to help the student master the language but also to put him at ease and to get him to talk freely with other members of the class. Pictures can open up an interesting exchange of personal experiences. For example, a picture is assigned to each of several small groups into which the class is divided. Members of each group are encouraged to examine the picture assigned and to share among themselves experiences from their own past that are recalled by the picture. This small-group sharing, valuable in itself, might well lead to the sharing of experiences with the entire class. Members of the class may bring pictures of their own to be shown in the opaque projector as they explain them.

When studied and discussed by the class, pictures showing American citizens carrying on their citizenship responsibilities, their everyday tasks, and their social activities provide understanding of our way of life and an opportunity for purposeful use of the English language.

HEALTH AND SAFETY

Pictures of physically fit individuals engaging in normal activities contrasted with those of unhealthy persons may be the means through which students discover that posture, bodily movement, emotional behavior, and grooming are important indexes to the state of one's health. This pictorial approach to the study of health can be modified to suit all age levels; at every age, pictures arouse interest and stimulate thoughtful questions.

Posture Study

Posture is a problem among all age groups. Pictures of acquired deformities and pictures and demonstrations of causative postural habits are useful in the primary grades as guidance materials to prevent postural difficulties. Study charts of the body framework and the work of muscles and tendons help boys and girls learn the significance of correct posture. X-ray photographs demonstrate the relationship between posture and the development of bone structure. Pictures showing faulty bone structure and its effect on the function of internal organs give emphasis to the need for good posture and prepare students to analyze intelligently pictures of standing, sitting, and sleeping postures.

Students of all age levels may make their own illustrations to show the *do*'s and *don't*'s of good posture. A primary group used stick figures to make a booklet, "Good Posture Can Be Fun." In a high school where posture was recognized as a problem, student-made posters and full-length mirrors were installed in school corridors. The poster messages reinforced by the sight of their own reflections brought about a great improvement in both teachers' and students' posture.

Pictures of corrective exercises aid learning in several ways: in preparation for demonstrations, they are studied to perfect procedures; during demonstrations, they are used to direct attention to key points; following demonstrations, they are displayed for ready reference.

The Body Frame

A person's appearance is determined to a great extent by the type of bone framework and muscular development he possesses. Each student should recognize his type of build and be encouraged to make the most of his appearance. Models, diagrams, and pictures of the structure and arrangement of muscles help a student recognize his type of body—its strong features, its weaknesses, and its needs. Collecting and organizing pictures showing muscular coordination and rhythmic motion make students more aware of activities for developing these skills.

By means of pictures, it is possible to present the whole array of activities that are open to those students barred from strenuous exercises because of physical disabilities. By judicious use of pictures that show persons like themselves happily engaging in permitted activities, discouraged students may be helped to a more positive approach to living with their disabilities. Study of pictures of proper and faulty procedures in stooping and lifting, accompanied by guided practice, prevents back injuries and the accompanying internal disturbances brought on by faulty procedures.

OFFICIALS OF THE
WORLD HEALTH ORGANIZATION
JUDGE STUDENT PICTURES
DESIGNED TO TEACH
BETTER DIET AND POSTURE HABITS.
(PHOTO: UNICEF)

Emotional Behavior

Students should understand the basic drives which are common to all. Pictures show how drives are put to work. For example, discussion of a chart on emotions initiated the collection of pictures to show how emotions are expressed at different maturity levels. The very act of collecting such pictures focused attention on evaluation of behavior and paved the way for more detailed study leading to selection of pictures that clearly demonstrated mature emotional responses.

Boys and girls should learn the meaning of emotional maturity. When basic needs are not adequately met, a child is less apt to "act his age." Even young children recognize temper tantrums as infantile behavior. By using pictures displayed for all to see and read, one teacher helped her fourth-grade class understand how taking care of their bodies would help them to act mature. Later, she displayed on feltboard a picture of a child in an outburst of temper and above it the caption, "You Won't Act Like This If ——." The children were asked to select from the group of accompanying pictures those indicating good health habits that would prevent a temper tantrum. Pictures were selected with such captions as "You Go to Bed on Time" and "You Eat a Good Breakfast." Finally, the class helped the teacher to arrange a display for demonstrating the idea to another fourth-grade group.

Social maturity is the theme of the well-illustrated book for teen-agers, *Your Manners Are Showing*.[2] Each page contains a color cartoon accompanied by a four-line jingle. Picture and jingle furnish effective material for individual and group guidance. Teen-age students have responded to this book by making a supplement of their own. Pages shown in an opaque projector from the original book or from the students' supplement will stimulate discussions on social success, diplomacy at home, and date problems.

In order to better understand emotional and social behavior, students must be taught the function of the endocrine glands. A diagram shows the location of these glands. A picture of the thyroid gland, for example, aids the teacher in explaining its function, significance, and signs of malfunction. Pictures will help the teacher or a member of the class explain what is involved in the metabolism test. Before-and-after pictures reveal the visible change in persons with advanced thyroid gland disturbances after they have had proper medical treatment.

By using pictures as targets for discussion, it is possible to analyze expressions of emotional behavior without embarrassing personal references. For example, a group of junior high-school students made original cartoons and posters showing how people meet such difficulties as procrastinating, alibiing, daydreaming, and depending on others for planning a course of action. In some junior and senior high schools, captioned pictorial charts are used for a discussion of the problems in expressing one's emotions and one's individuality. The charts are accompanied by a list of questions to stimulate thought.

Good Grooming

Personal hygiene may be approached from the standpoint of good grooming. By means of pictures, teachers can demonstrate care of the skin, nails, and hair. Pictures enable boys and girls to discover what contributes to and detracts from the well-groomed look. Through study and discussion, they will discover that health and cleanliness are essential to the well-groomed appearance. Pictures and charts

---

[2] Betz, Betty. *Your Manners Are Showing*. New York: Grosset & Dunlap, 1946. 95 p.

acquaint them with the work of the dentist and the optometrist and with their own role in dental and eye care. Pictures of foods which help to build sound teeth or are harmful to the teeth, along with pictures of healthy and diseased teeth, add interest and emphasis.

Attention should be given to purchases necessary for good grooming. By combining information in *Consumer Reports* with a pictorial display of products, young people learn how to choose inexpensive, harmless, and effective cosmetics, deodorants, and soaps. Pictures collected as examples of clothing appropriate for school and social occasions, accompanied by information on materials and prices, are also valuable.

Nutrition

Some aspects of nutrition can be studied effectively through pictures. Posters showing a well-balanced breakfast introduce a comparison between the food the members of a group ate and the model meal shown in the picture. Cutouts of foods may be arranged on feltboard for individuals to select items for a meal and give reasons for their choices. Organizing pictures of foods into those rich in various nutrients is an excellent method for review.

Pictures of persons with pellagra, rickets, and other vitamin-deficiency diseases, along with pictures of them following a period of adequate diet, are successful arguments for good eating habits. "Food Made the Difference" is a good caption for this display.

Organs of the Body

Pictures may be used for showing how the organs of the body function. While a model serves better than any other teaching tool for studying the parts of the heart, a large wall chart or a small diagram shown in an opaque projector makes it possible to see how the maze of veins and arteries work together to sustain life. The double picture spread in *World Book Encyclopedia*, "Wonders of the Heart,"[3] contains eight facts about the heart. Though the pages are too crowded for study all at once, the wise teacher will use the illustrations one at a time in the opaque projector.

Although a model is best for teaching about the digestive system, a picture may be used successfully here, too. If, as discussion proceeds, the picture is laid out part by part on feltboard, attention is

---

[3] Jones, J. Morris, editor. *World Book Encyclopedia*. Chicago: Field Enterprises Educational Corporation, 1961. Vol. 8, p. 136-37.

directed specifically to one part at a time as it is introduced verbally into the sequence.

Disease

As children mature they should become familiar with the work done by their local, county, state, and federal departments of health. It is a first step toward developing the insight that must be theirs if they are to become adult citizens properly concerned over matters of public health. Toward this end, a bulletin board could be assembled titled "An Ounce of Prevention," with pictures arranged to show that a quarantine prevented an epidemic and a chest X-ray prevented a long stay in a tuberculosis sanitorium. Such a display may also serve as a good introduction to the study of communicable diseases and to an appreciation of preventive measures enforced by public-health regulations.

Class committees may take trips to get firsthand information about the services of community, public, and philanthropic health and welfare agencies. When committees share their information with the class, pictures may be used on feltboard or in the opaque projector to spotlight key ideas and to enliven reports. Pictures selected to show how milk is made pure and safe for the consumer would make the subject of food inspection significant. A display—"Do You Know These Microbe Hunters?"—is a good introduction to the film, *Immunization*,[4] which, in turn, is followed by a picture display, "When Epidemic Threatens." Since students must agree among themselves on the measures to be followed in a public-health emergency, this assignment would stimulate critical thinking.

As a part of the study of communicable diseases, students might arrange companion bulletin boards, "Methods of Transmitting Diseases" and "Methods of Preventing Diseases." Original sketches and collected pictures would serve as a visual summary to point up a final discussion of disease prevention.

For the study of degenerative diseases, a bulletin board would direct attention to the work of such agencies as cancer clinics and the National Heart Association. A chart indicating the common areas of cancer attack would be used for a discussion of symptoms. Pictures to demonstrate how people overtax the heart—"Does *Your* Heart Find *You* Guilty?"—might initiate study of proper care of the heart. Pictures collected by students to show common methods of treatment for heart disease, along with pictures of activities permitted the cooperative patient, would encourage each student to act in the best interests of his heart.

Through use of silhouettes, photographs, and illustrations, students become acquainted with methods of medical treatment. As they acquire familiarity with treatment methods, they become less apprehensive about the unknown and gain respect and admiration for the advances made in medical science during this century.

Health Insurance

Paying for medical care is an important part of the health problem. A bulletin board planned to show outstanding features of low-cost medical care would direct attention to this problem. By taking a health insurance policy and showing pictorially what benefits are guaranteed under certain conditions, students discover how to read health and accident policies and evaluate them intelligently.

Pictures of elderly persons living actively, contrasted with others unhappy and alone, might encourage students to investigate the

---

[4] *Immunization*. 11 min., 16mm, sound, b & w. Encyclopedia Britannica Films, 1150 Wilmette Avenue, Wilmette, Illinois, 1955.

problem of care for the aged. Pictures selected to use with a panel discussion, "We Plan for a Happy Old Age," might illustrate (a) preserving healthy bodies, (b) developing skills and hobby interests, (c) making friends and keeping in touch, (d) investigating retirement plans, and (e) developing an adequate insurance program.

Safety Programs

The school program on safety can be introduced and developed through the study of pictures. Young children learn much by preparing their own series of pictures to demonstrate a safe day. These pictures, mounted on a long roll of shelf paper, can be shown in the opaque projector (one pupil unrolling enough for each exposure; another, rolling up the opposite portion) for an elementary-school assembly program. A student committee discusses the pictures as they appear on the screen.

At every age level, the importance of safety becomes more significant when students take an active part in the selection of displays for safety reminders. In one senior high school, driver education classes make up original slogans which they illustrate and post throughout the school building prior to long holiday weekends.

THIS LIVELY DISCUSSION OF THE SCHOOL SAFETY PROGRAM IS CENTERED ON A PICTORIAL REPRESENTATION OF DANGER SPOTS IN THE SCHOOL ENVIRONMENT. (PHOTO: STANDARD OIL CO., N. J.)

These safety reminders in strategic places in the school building do much toward making the student body safety-conscious.

For supplementation and enrichment, pictures may be combined with demonstrations on safety. For example, pictures of accidents in the home, at school, and on the street may accompany a dramatic skit. In a primary-grade group a photograph showing the collision of two boys in a school corridor, causing damage to a pottery bowl which took several hours to repair, was shown in an opaque projector. As the picture was displayed, the teacher commented, "That accident did not just happen. It could have been prevented." When she turned off the projector, she permitted volunteers to show just how. A group of three boys—playing the two boys and a commentator—held a conference, then quickly took their places. As the two boys approached from opposite directions the commentator said, "Notice, neither boy is rushing too fast, and both are watching where they're going." For the next skit, 10 children, with a narrator, separated into two groups. As the two groups approached each other from opposite directions, the narrator called attention to the fact that there could be no collisions because each one was keeping to the right, watching where he was going, and remembering to walk, not run.

In a sixth-grade class a child brought in a newspaper picture showing a boy's battered bicycle, the spot where the boy had been thrown, and an automobile rammed into a telephone pole in an effort to miss the boy. Following a discussion, the class worked out a dramatization of bicycle safety for an all-school assembly program. The program, "Accidents Don't Just Happen—There's Always a Cause," was introduced by the newspaper picture.

First Aid

Studying pictures of techniques for bandaging and other first-aid measures may precede and guide actual practice sessions and stimulate thoughtful discussion. When pictures of conditions requiring the immediate services of a physician are analyzed along with others showing conditions requiring first-aid measures, students develop a basis for intelligent discrimination.

HOME ECONOMICS

Education for family life and for homemaking begins when the child becomes a member of the family group, but much specific knowledge and experience for successful homemaking can be gained only in school. Though most school instruction ultimately makes a student a better homemaker, it is the homemaking teacher who presents the greatest body of practical material useful in homemaking and family life.

For instruction, a home economics teacher uses pictures as well as objects, demonstrations, and laboratory work. She frequently finds that young people understand principles best when they see something tangible, and that seeing usually precedes knowledge or understanding. In all areas that focus on family well-being, she finds many applications for pictures.

Family Relationships

The homemaking teacher may have a collection of pictures showing family situations and problems for the class to look at and discuss. Pictures showing young people in problem situations with parents, with grandparents, and with other siblings stimulate the class to a discussion that is impersonal yet has individual application. Take, for example, a picture of an eighth grader trying on a new party dress before the mirror as she is watched closely, but somewhat apprehensively, by her little sister. The class may observe, "The girl is showing her sister her new dress"; ask, "Why does the little girl look so worried?"; or answer, "Sometimes big sisters don't want little sisters around and they say mean things to them." The teacher might follow with, "What is the little girl learning as she watches her sister?" The discussion may lead to ideas on feminine roles and how they are learned, relationships of the underdog to those in authority, or sibling relationships.

Child Development

Because teen-agers are the baby sitters in our society, they are confronted with problems of child development in their everyday living. A bulletin board, "What the Baby Sitter Needs To Know," would focus attention on problems to be studied. For example, a picture that shows an emotional disturbance usually contains cues to the cause of the incident and the manner in which it is handled. Students gain much from analyzing the picture and participating in a guided discussion of the effect on a child of different methods for solving the problem.

Pictures are valuable also for reference or reminder following a demonstration. For example, after observing a demonstration of

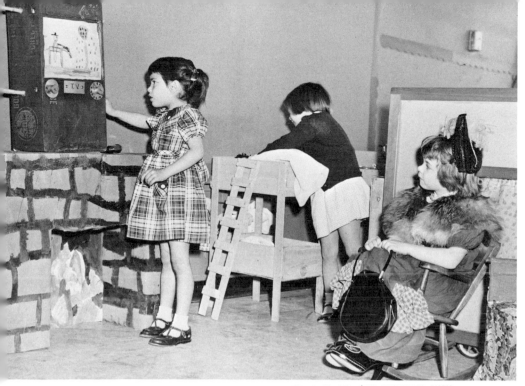

EDUCATION FOR FAMILY LIVING BEGINS EARLY, AND PICTURES SUCH AS THIS PROVIDE BOTH TEACHERS AND CHILDREN WITH IDEAS FOR DRAMATIZED LEARNING ACTIVITIES. (PHOTO: PALO ALTO (CALIF.) UNIFIED SCHOOL DISTRICT)

toys and games suitable for young children, members of a class cut up old mail-order catalogs and arranged pictures of toys according to the age levels for which they were best suited.

Pictures of children engaged in everyday activities are helpful for learning behavior characteristics of children at different ages. The pictures stimulate discussion and point up what to look for when the students observe or baby-sit with children.

Safety and First Aid

Because such a large proportion of the accidents reported annually occur in the home, eliminating home accidents is of tremendous importance. A series of bulletin boards arranged by class committees goes far toward making the girls aware of methods for accident prevention. For example, one bulletin board might demonstrate "The Do's and Don't's in Handling Electrical Equipment" and another might show "Common Causes of Falls."

Today's baby sitters and tomorrow's homemakers should learn the basic fundamentals of first aid. How to care for cuts and burns and what to do until the doctor comes are two of the many situations where pictures showing step-by-step procedures can be used to demonstrate and clarify details.

Interior Decoration

The study of home furnishings is an excellent example of how pictures often serve the demonstrator's purpose far better than the use of actual materials. Selected pictures demonstrate color effects in a room by providing material for a study of the same room done in several different decorating schemes. Through use of inexpensive pictures, clipped from furniture advertising brochures and periodicals such as *Woman's Day* and *Better Homes and Gardens,* the teacher can give instruction on how to identify styles of furniture, judge quality when purchasing furniture, and arrange furniture. Arrangement of wall pictures for home decoration and styles of lamps, curtains, and draperies for different windows are made clear through pictures.

Suppose the problem is to choose a chair for a specific wall space in a living room. To be considered are the size of the chair in relation to the size of the room, the wall space to be occupied, harmony with other furnishings, purpose, sturdiness, design, kind and quality of the wood, and the durability of the upholstery. To direct attention to the structure of the chair, the teacher introduces pictures of types of joints. Careful study reveals why the spiral grooved pin or the mortised and tenoned joint insures a durability impossible to achieve with the use of nails or glue. Similar analysis of pictures would help students understand why straight legs of a chair may split if the grain does not follow the length of the leg. To develop taste in decorating, the teacher shows a picture of a room with oversized furniture in contrast to a room with well-scaled furniture or a picture of a room where the style or color of a chair is out of harmony and ruins an otherwise pleasing effect.

Home Management

Pictures help in the teaching of household management. Scale drawings and diagrammatic pictures furnish material for analyzing the efficiency of kitchen arrangements. As a preparation for intelligent stocking of supplies, student committees assemble pictorial displays to show the linens or the kitchen utensils for a family of two.

Pictures are important for illustrating table setting, flower arrangement, and choice of linens, dishes, and flatware. Examples of the relationship among the menu, the type of service, and the table arrangement are shown much more easily through a collection of pictures than by actual example.

Consumer Buying

It is important for the individual and for society that students (especially girls) in the schools learn to be intelligent buyers. In our country, the women do more than 85 percent of the nation's retail buying. While major purchases are usually made by the women only after consultation with their husbands, it is they who shop around to find the best buy. Since women carry so much responsibility for consumer buying, it is important that they be prepared for the task.

Advertisements, especially those in women's magazines, are a good starting point. Advertisements of different brands of the same item might be compared and analyzed to alert students to considerations basic to making value judgments. An advertisement in *Good Housekeeping* might be compared with another of the same product in *Esquire.* Such study would reveal how a sales pitch varies from one audience to another.

Dress and Grooming

In one home economics class, photographs of women in public life served to focus attention on good grooming. In another class the teacher introduced a unit on dress and grooming with a set of photographs, "The Sorry Sue Series." This series includes pictures of Sue as the overdressed girl at an informal party; Sue as the target for criticism after she appeared on the bus with her hair in pin curls; and Sue in a wrinkled blouse and soiled gloves. These pictures were a stimulus for a discussion of the selection of clothes for assorted occasions and of the habit of good grooming.

One class divided into committees to take up problems of dress and grooming. Two girls in one group took close-up shots, in color, of finger nails to reveal the care given to them. Another committee clipped pictures from magazines for a series of charts, "What's the Occasion?" On each chart were samples of dress appropriate for specific occasions. A third committee used the title, "Fact, Figure, and Fashion" for dramatized interviews in which one girl presented a problem to two experts. Using prepared sketches and a few stage props, the experts handled such problems as what hair style and neckline is most suited to a specific facial shape.

Sewing

A study picture used prior to a film showing enables students to view the film with greater interest and purpose. For example, as

MAGAZINES TODAY CONTAIN MANY FINE PICTURES OF FOODS, AND
THESE CHILDREN HAVE USED THEM WITH MEANING TO ILLUSTRATE A
REPORT TO THEIR CLASS ON DIET ESSENTIALS. (PHOTO: PALO ALTO
(CALIF.) UNIFIED SCHOOL DISTRICT)

preparation for the film, *Sewing: Characteristics and Handling Materials*,[5] one teacher showed pictures of two persons wearing dresses of the same striped material cut from the same pattern—one, where the seamstress had used the stripes to advantage; the other, where the stripes failed to match. Other pictures revealed how a dress with good basic design was ruined by cheap and excessive trimming. Students suggested a simple trim that would add quality and style to the dress.

Foods and Nutrition

Color charts and pictures used on feltboard are excellent aids for learning about food; they add interest and realism to problems on nutrition. For example, shown the main course of a meal, students are asked to choose, among many pictures, an accompanying salad and dessert, with reasons for their choice. Displays on feltboard of food combinations for regular and special diets also make possible evaluation of food combinations for nutritive value and eye appeal.

---

[5] *Sewing: Characteristics and Handling Materials*. 10 min., 16mm, sound, b & w. Young America Films, 18 East 41st Street, New York 17, New York, 1948.

A series of bulletin boards arranged by student committees on the problem of storage and cooking of fresh foods reveal how these processes affect nutritive value. Research and discussion by committee members as they select and arrange material for a bulletin board, "Meat from Market Basket to Table," prepares them for leadership in class discussion of the topic. The bulletin board furnishes a visual procedure for analysis and discussion.

Pictures of foods that are good seasonal buys will alert students to one way of saving money. Charts showing cuts of meat illustrate which cuts are good buys—nutritionally equivalent, yet less expensive than other cuts.

THE LANGUAGE ARTS

The basic purpose of the language arts program is to improve communication. In the subject-matter-centered program, the language arts encompass the formal subjects of dramatics, speech, language, spelling, oral and written expression, semantics, reading, and literature. In the experience-centered program, all aspects of the language arts are explored by the learners as needs and interests arise. To describe how pictures assist in the teaching of language arts in either program, this chapter has been divided into the categories of oral expression, written expression, and reading and literature.

Oral Expression

Pictures play a role in oral communication by creating an atmosphere. A room made cheerful by a few well-selected pictures helps children to become relaxed and ready to talk. If, on their first day in school, children are greeted by picture displays of other young children happily engaged in familiar activities, they will feel more secure and comfortable—here is a place where people know and like children. Following the summer holiday, pictures of vacation activities may encourage exchanges of personal experiences and help students find mutual interests.

Photographs or pictures of families, homes, pets, and activities encourage young children to speak, listen, and look. Young children enjoy drawing pictures of their own homes. Their sketches may point up differences in types of dwellings. The teacher then uses illustrations of apartment houses and one-family houses to clarify concepts and to prepare children for a walking trip to see types of houses in the neighborhood.

Following the planned visit of a child's pet to school, the teacher may select pictures to focus attention on the care of pets. By choosing pictures which emphasize the key idea, *care,* she helps children to look with a purpose and to organize ideas.

Pictures may be used to enrich storytelling. One method is to select a picture and encourage children to offer some interpretation before the teacher relates the story. This procedure helps children to progress beyond simply seeing objects and encourages them to draw inferences. Suppose the teacher selects a picture showing a small boy running from a house toward a man who is removing a large package from a parked car. She might begin by saying, "Here is Jack. Before I relate the story, maybe some of you will tell me what you think the story will be." Observations may be: "Jack wants to see who the man is." "The man is delivering a package." "No, he's not; that's not a delivery truck." "Jack's uncle is bringing him a present." "This is Jack's birthday and his father is bringing him a gift." "Jack's father has come home from work and Jack and his father have a surprise for his mother." At this point, the teacher may establish the fact that it is Jack's birthday and ask what time of year it is. The children will note that Jack's father is wearing a topcoat, Jack is wearing corduroys, and the tree in the yard has shed its leaves. Such use of pictures not only stimulates oral expression but also teaches picture interpretation and provides specific purposes for listening.

Well-selected pictures are excellent aids to speech correction. The child who needs exercises in speech may lose self-consciousness and actually enjoy identifying pictures of objects, composing suitable captions for pictures, or relating the story of a picture. Such pictures also add interest to exercises for children with speech and hearing problems.

Students should have access to pictures for use in oral reports and assigned speeches. For example, a student assigned to speak in class about his travels decided to tell of the Italian *palio* he had attended. By use of a diagrammatic sketch, enlarged in an opaque projector, he prepared his listeners for a full appreciation of picture post cards of the event. The pictures helped his audience to catch the spirit of this traditional contest, still held in all its medieval pomp and pageantry.

The teacher of dramatics is interested in training students to use all means of expression: voice, words, eyes, face, gestures, clothing,

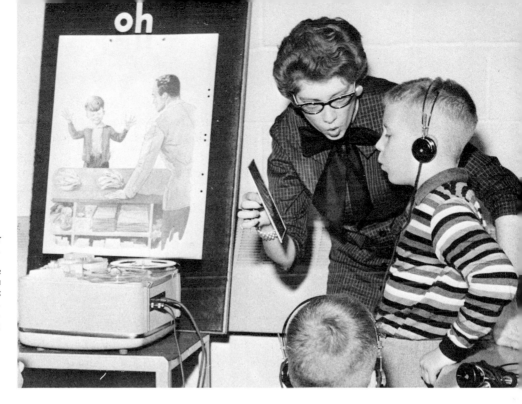

and posture. Well-selected pictures can provide experience in analyzing methods of expressing emotions and states of mind. The teacher who asks students to collect pictures of facial expressions, hands, and other physical manifestations of emotions finds that they enter wholeheartedly into the activity and become increasingly discerning in discussing and organizing their collection.

For every dramatic production—from simple role playing, when children dress up in old clothes found in the attic, to the most ambitious of senior high-school productions—student actors want their representations to be as authentic as possible. To achieve authenticity of dress, scenery, and stage properties, it is wise to consult encyclopedias, illustrated books, and costume plates in commercial picture sets. Students will check one source against another until they have adequate designs for the costumes.

In a class where faulty usage was the rule rather than the exception, the teacher was able to capture the interest of the students and challenge them by use of cartoon sketches. A few poorly constructed sentences were selected from a set of compositions. One of the selections was "Barking ferociously at his reflection in the mirror, Jim hastily loaded his camera and took the amusing picture of his pup that won the prize." Sketches were made to dramatize the precise meaning of the sentences as they were written. Students were soon vying with one another to be the first to recognize an error that could be sketched amusingly. When ambiguity and loose sentence structure became a target for discussion, members of the class began to work assiduously to eliminate errors from their own work before others discovered them.

Written Expression

Pictures play an integral part in promoting written expression. The very young child communicates his ideas by making an original drawing accompanied by a simple caption or title. Older children include as part of their compositions photographs taken for the purpose of clarifying, supplementing, or adding interest to specific passages. It is important that students spot places where an illustration, no matter how simple, will add interest and clarity to written expression. They must have access to picture files and be encouraged to select pictures both as basic sources of information and as aids to communication.

Pictures may serve as a review or reminder and as an aid to organization of ideas for written expression. For example, in a fifth-grade class the teacher used pictures for children to discover the advantages of preplanning or outlining in preparation for written expression. She selected "The Story of Milk" because it was familiar to all members of the group and because it was being studied in the second grade where the accounts written by fifth graders would be read with interest. The fifth graders enjoyed the challenge of writing for others. To help them, the teacher introduced a picture display. Each picture was marked with an easy-to-see letter of the alphabet. Every member of the class was asked to look at the pictures, to indicate the sequence of pictured ideas he would use in his composition (B-F-A, C-A-E, etc.), and to explain his reason for the arrangement chosen. Once the class actually began writing, work was much easier. One boy exclaimed, "Why writing's simple this way. I know what I want to say."

To encourage creative expression the teacher often must help children discover that they have something to write. The skillful teacher will also be alert to possibilities for developing appreciation of literature. The teacher will select pleasing phrases, short descriptions, and interesting titles to share with the students and to interest them in looking themselves. Such sharing builds readiness for the use of pictures to stimulate writing.

A teacher assigned a sixth-grade class to write the part of a story which one of several pictures suggested. One of the pictures was of a boy about 10 years old eagerly grasping a football, which apparently had been given to him by a man between the ages of 30 and 40. Both were standing in a modestly furnished room. The picture stimulated the following written responses:

The boy took the ball in both hands.

John shouted, "Oh boy!" as he grabbed the new football from his dad.

Dick was so happy that he didn't see anything but the football, which he eagerly grabbed in both hands. You couldn't tell who was happier, Dick or his grinning father.

Dave just stood clutching the new football in both hands. It was real and it was his. He hoped to find exactly the right words to thank his "big brother," a friend who knew how to make his tenth birthday his happiest one.

Both Bill and his father grinned happily. They seemed to understand each other even if they didn't know each other very well. As Bill fondly held the football in both hands he wondered if his father also was wishing that they could try it out together.

WHAT WOULD YOUR STUDENTS TELL US ABOUT THEMSELVES IF THEY WERE ASKED TO WRITE TITLES, CAPTION STORIES, OR COMPOSE POEMS ABOUT THESE PICTURES?

Another picture, a colored print of a sunset, stimulated the following:

Evening, clad in a cool dark coat, steals in quietly
As daylight bows out,
Gloriously clad in her changeable taffeta gown.

A red ball o'er the horizon's bluish rim,
The sun is setting
O'er the great waste of dark blue water.

The sunset was dressed in orange that night
With a violet pinned at her waist,
And, at her feet, her flowing robe
Was the surf of a giant wave.

Reading and Literature

Skillful teaching makes learning to read an adventure. In building reading readiness, the teacher uses pictures to develop a meaningful vocabulary, arouse interest and curiosity, and aid in discovering cues to content of the stories to be read aloud. When children begin reading, the teacher continues to use pictures. Her questions prompt the children to relate the new words to the pictures. For example, when a child fails to recognize the phrase "on the corner," the teacher may inquire, "Where is Officer Murphy standing?"

As children progress through the grades, the teacher uses pictures to make an interesting reading corner. The illustrated poems or the display of book jackets which the teacher arranges may alternate with displays of newly discovered books or children's creative efforts. A second-grade class made a mural of their interpretation of a favorite story. On the sixth-grade level a wall hanging of the group's favorite book characters pointed up the reading center.

At times, a poem can best be understood by aid of a picture. For example, Oliver Wendell Holmes' "The Chambered Nautilus" is meaningful only when the reader has been prepared by study and discussion of a picture showing a cross section of a nautilus shell. In Carl Sandburg's "Washington Monument at Night," an artist's interpretation of a poem is useful to the reader. Unless the illustrator is also the author, however, a teacher should make clear that another person's interpretation is being introduced. For emphasis, it is good to have the students themselves think of pictures for the poem and compare them with that of the illustrator.

In one class, a student reported on the life and works of John Masefield. To add interest, he showed three pictures and played excerpts from a recording of Masefield's poetry.

IN THIS CLASSROOM, PICTURES LITERALLY FORM THE BACKGROUND FOR A STUDY OF SHAKESPEARE. NOTE THAT SCENES FROM ACTUAL PRODUCTIONS LEND A DRAMATIC TOUCH TO THE MORE STAID POR- TRAITS OF THE BARD. (PHOTO. CARL PURCELL, NEA)

To fully understand a work of literature, students must know some- thing of the background against which the work was written. Pictures are indispensable for building background.

To understand Shakespeare, for example, students should see pictures of the city of London during his lifetime and the theater in which his plays were produced. Only through such picture study can students appreciate that Shakespeare produced plays specifically for his time and for the Globe Theater. In addition, Shakespeare's plays should be presented to students by means of film and recordings. When a film or recording of a play is used, study prints showing staging of the same play in the Memorial Theater at Stratford-on-Avon or in other theaters in the United States and Canada are valuable for comparison and contrast.

Many novelists are greatly influenced by the life and times in which they write. Illustrations of social conditions and cartoons from periodicals of their day aid in understanding the work of authors such as Charles Dickens and Harriet Beecher Stowe. Also, such pictures serve as a touchstone for judging the validity of the authors' approach.

Some authors work specifically to portray their own life and times. To appreciate fully Clarence Day's *Life with Father,* a humorous account of life in the Gay Nineties, the teacher should introduce pictures showing the dress, home furnishings, manners, and customs of the period.

Without the use of well-selected pictures, much of the drama and realism of autobiography and biography are lost. For the study of these forms of narrative, pictures superimposed on a time line are helpful. The span of the subject's life becomes the time line and on it are pictorial representations of outstanding events during his lifetime. A time line of H. L. Mencken's life, for example, would indicate, in addition to the major events in his life, contemporary affairs which influenced him and fellow writers with whom he was closely associated.

MUSIC

In a song, the word *chimney sweep* so confused a fourth-grade boy that he said, "The words don't make any sense at all. Besides, who ever heard of calling a chimney swift a chimney sweep?" Only after she overheard this comment did the teacher take time to discover that not a single member of the class knew the meaning of the word. Her attempts at a verbal explanation were unsatisfactory. Therefore, on the following day she made use of three pictures: a chimney sweep with the tools of his trade, chimneys on the roof tops of London, and a chimney swift. The interested response to her belated use of pictures awakened the teacher to the necessity of anticipating need for this form of instruction.

The search for appropriate pictures is a time-consuming task for the teacher of music because commercial producers of teaching pictures have not done much in this area. However, the resourceful teacher locates many pictures in professional journals, illustrated books, post card collections, sets of pictures designed for teaching about ethnic and social groups, and advertisements and brochures issued by leading producers of records and musical instruments.

Musical Instruments

Ideally, when acquainting students with an unfamiliar musical instrument, the teacher arranges for them to see and hear it played correctly. However, it is usually possible to arrange for demonstrating only the more common instruments. A good picture of an instrument—the harp, for example—as it is being played correctly, accompanied by a sound recording, provides a good substitute for a demonstration. By using an opaque projector, the image of the player and the instrument become life-size. As children become acquainted with the harp, they may be encouraged to start a collection of instruments with which they are familiar.

A permanent wall chart is effective for preparing listeners to locate instruments as they are arranged in an orchestra. An excellent wall chart found in the book, *This Is the Orchestra*,[6] is excellent for use in an opaque projector.

Music with Words

Pictures can help to establish the mood and bring to life the setting for many songs. In preparation for the teaching of "Naples" and "Neapolitan Boat Song," a teacher selected three pictures in color: a daylight view of the Bay of Naples, with the city and Mount Vesuvius in the distance; a close-up of a festival of Naples; and a view of the Bay of Naples in moonlight. Through study of these pictures, the group caught the spirit of the songs

Pictures are invaluable for reference. When young people make plans for performing an operetta—an original production or a favorite work such as *H.M.S. Pinafore*—they should be given access to pictures for gathering data essential for developing appropriate costumes and scenery.

Pictures can add considerably to students' appreciation of the works of a composer. In the case of Stephen Foster, such songs of his as "My Old Kentucky Home" and "Old Folks at Home" become more enjoyable when the teacher displays pictures of the scenes that may have suggested their writing.

Foster's "Oh! Susanna" and "Camptown Races" were composed for minstrel shows. Pictures of these shows, if available, are good to exhibit. Also, introduction of a picture of the forty-niners gathered about their campfire singing "Oh! Susanna," with the information that it was selected as their marching song, might well stimulate a new listening to catch the spirit of the song which gave it special appeal to the pioneers of the West.

---

[6] Posell, Elsa Z. *This Is the Orchestra*. Boston: Houghton Mifflin Co., 1950. p. 13-14.

Composers

Outstanding musicians—instrumentalists, conductors, or composers—may become interesting individuals to students or they may never be more than names that seemed important to the teacher. Pictures often make the difference. They help students to feel some kinship with great musicians. But, pictures must be judiciously selected. A bust portrait of the individual or a picture of the exterior of his home does not captivate the interest or stir the imagination. To acquaint young people with a musician, it is necessary to select pictures of interesting episodes in his life.

In the case of Mozart, elementary-school pupils would be interested in seeing a winter view of the place of his birth—the Austrian town of Salzburg, located at the foot of a mountain with a gray stone castle high above it on the mountainside. An illustration of the baby who was christened Joannes Chrysostomus Wolfgangus Theophilus Mozart appeals to children. Other pictures of interest are: the three-year-old boy counting, *"einz, zwie, drei,"* and beating time with his fists as he listens to music; the four-year-old sitting at the clavier where he learned a minuet in half an hour; Mozart at the age of five composing his "Minuet in G." A good book to use in class

VISUAL REFERENCES TO BRASS INSTRUMENTS ALREADY DEMONSTRATED, THESE LARGE PICTURES, MOUNTED ON HEAVY BOARDS, ARE AN IMPORTANT PART OF THIS LESSON FOR FUTURE BANDSMEN. (PHOTO: FRO "A CAREER IN MUSIC EDUCATION, PUBLISHED BY MUSIC EDUCATORS NATIONAL CONFERENCE)

is *Mozart the Wonder Boy*.[7] It is well illustrated and contains excerpts from a number of his compositions.

More mature pupils are drawn to the young Mozart who was stopped by murmuring in the audience while playing at a concert in Naples—his listeners thought the ring that flashed as he played held the secret to his performance. A picture of the young artist removing the ring to prove that it provided no magic touch would catch the attention of the class. Also effective is a picture of Mozart listening to the service "Tenebree" in Rome's Sistine Chapel. Music for this service was never seen by anyone except the performers. Mozart heard it once, wrote it out from memory, and returned again to a performance to check his few errors. When his remarkable feat became known, his transcription was requested and a comparison with the actual score revealed every note to be correct. Also of interest is a picture of Mozart asleep from the fatigue of working to finish the overture to *Don Giovanni* for its presentation the following day. This picture, followed by one of the young conductor-composer only a few

---

[7] Wheeler, O., and Dencher, S. *Mozart the Wonder Boy*. Revised edition. New York: E. P. Dutton & Co., 1941. 127 p.

hours later taking his place to conduct the first performance of the opera, would be impressive. While these two pictures reveal part of Mozart's personal story, they are essentially part of the story of every creative artist.

Music Projects

A study of the development of jazz grew out of a pictorial exhibit arranged by a committee of eleventh graders to teach highbrows (classmates who looked with disdain on jazz enthusiasts) about jazz. Under the guidance of the teacher, the entire class listened critically to various forms of music for purposes of comparison. In the process, respect for individual taste and preference increased considerably.

Pictures stimulate interest in forthcoming musical events. In one school, committees from music groups—band, chorus, glee club, orchestra—assume responsibility for turning a large corridor bulletin board into an up-to-date bait board. To advertise Marian Anderson's appearance on television, for example, highlights of her career were visually presented on the board, and one of her recordings was played over the school's public address system.

SCIENCE

The science experiences of today's children and youth should prepare them to solve problems in their environment—and not only to solve problems, but to think critically and arrive at solutions in a truly scientific manner. When teachers accept the necessity to provide these experiences, they become concerned with attitudes, critical thinking, and interest and appreciation, as well as with the acquisition of basic skills. In science study, pictures—alone or in conjunction with other materials of instruction—help students to define problems, experiment scientifically, observe, report, and interpret.

The Study of Animals

The need to care for a classroom pet interests students in the study of domestic animals. Children can begin by placing markers in books and clipping from advertisements the pictures which demonstrate the care of pets. As they participate in evaluating and grouping these pictures, pupils learn to organize materials. On some maturity levels, the teacher may encourage members of the class to consider how animals live in their natural habitats. Pictures can be shown of animals in the burrows, thickets, trees, and streams in which they live.

In a sixth-grade class a teacher arranged a display, "What Do *You* Collect?" On the board were pictures of a boy arranging his mineral collection and a girl capturing a butterfly with her net. The class brought in their own collections to share with each other. The first problem they encountered was one of organization. They began by grouping the collections into living and nonliving things, but classifying a starfish baffled some members of this group of inland children. This problem led the teacher to use pictures emphasizing growth and reproduction as characteristics of living organisms. Organisms were then divided into animal and plant groups and into subdivisions within each group.

For the continued study of animals, in grade school and in junior high school, pictures and pictorial charts have been used as aids in learning—

1. To supplement first-hand study of structural characteristics, such as the differences in the claws and bills of birds.

2. To furnish sufficient examples for children to make generalizations on animal adaptations to environment.

ANIMAL PICTURES COME ALIVE IN THIS FIFTH-GRADE CLASS, WHERE PICTURES HAVE PLAYED AN IMPORTANT ROLE IN CONCEPT DEVELOPMENT. (PHOTO: CLEVELAND PUBLIC SCHOOLS)

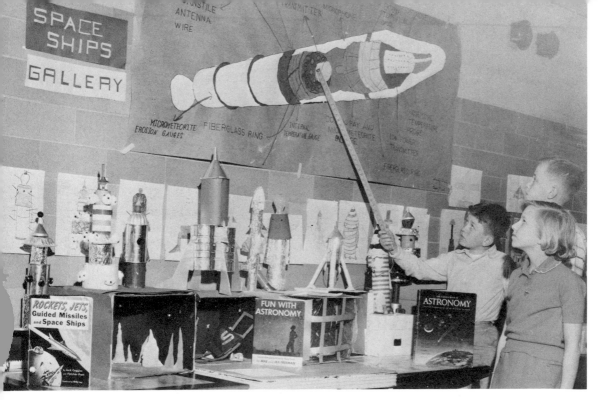

PICTURES, STUDENT MADE AND OTHERWISE, ARE ESSENTIAL TOOLS IN THE RAPIDLY CHANGING SCIENCE CURRICULUM. (PHOTO: WELLESLEY (MASS.) PUBLIC SCHOOLS)

3. To help students recognize nature's use of protective coloring.

4. To help students understand the community life of bees and to show similarities and differences in their community organization with that of ants and termites.

5. To compare pictures of the life cycle of the toad with children's first-hand observation of toads in the classroom and to compare their life cycle with that of frogs.

6. To extend the concept of the life cycle by contrasting the monarch butterfly or silkworm with the toad.

7. To aid in defining and extending the meaning of group labels, such as amphibian.

8. To compare pictures of the day-by-day changes in the chick embryo with a group's experimental findings on incubated eggs.

9. To demonstrate inheritance patterns so that inherited characteristics take on significance.

10. To help children appreciate the contributions of scientists such as those of Gregor Mendel, father of modern heredity theory.

The Study of Fossils

Pictures give reality and substance to things of the past. A fossil imbedded in a piece of limestone brought to class by a fourth-grade boy was used by his teacher as the starting point for a study of the forces which change the earth's surface. The group investigated the changes brought about during the Ice Age by a glacier which had penetrated their section of Ohio. Pictures were essential for building an understanding of the characteristics of a glacier. Pictures were used to extend the concept of fossils; they were necessary for conceptualizing what this part of the earth must have been like prior to the Ice Age. Across the back wall of the classroom, the class made a time line to show the earth's epochs from the Ice Age to the present. They illustrated the time line with a mural showing the animals and vegetation of various ages. As the group investigated the forces that have changed the earth's surface, they made detailed study of pictures of Virginia's Natural Bridge and Niagara Falls, examples of wind and water erosion, along with diagrams demonstrating the erosion process.

Scientific Procedure

Pictures may be used for recordkeeping and for the validation of group findings. For example, a first-grade class made a dated picture record of the growth and development of two mice, which

THIS PICTURE OF FOUR ATLAS INTERCONTINENTAL BALLISTIC MISSILE TANKS UNDER CONSTRUCTION IS ONE OF A SERIES OF SCHOOL STUDY PRINTS PREPARED BY THE SUPERINTENDENT OF SCHOOLS, SAN DIEGO COUNTY, CALIFORNIA. (PHOTO: CONVAIR DIVISION OF GENERAL DYNAMICS CORP.)

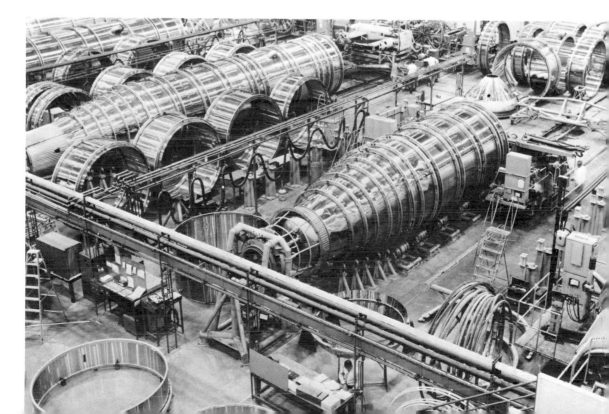

sustained interest, provided purpose and incentive for careful observation, and built respect for properly documented records. Pictures
served a similar purpose in a seventh-grade class where a documentary
record of the embryonic development of the chick was made by
photographing findings when an incubated egg was opened for study
each day. The completed record was compared with a similar record
on a commercially produced chart, and found to be typical and complete enough to serve as reliable for purposes of generalization and
review.

Scientific Investigation

The alert teacher uses picture study to raise questions and direct
attention to the need for scientific investigation. Having noted in his
seventh-grade class that a boy showed faith in a rabbit's foot and a
girl was frightened over having broken the mirror in her compact, one
teacher arranged a display of pictures representing some common
beliefs of possible causes of good and bad luck. From class discussion
it became evident that opinions on superstitions varied. Under teacher
guidance the class set up experiments to test the validity of beliefs
selected for examination.

Scientific Principles in Action

Children of all ages are interested in machines. The kindergarten
child operates his miniature crane to see what it will do and identifies
pictures of other complex machines. The fourth grader draws conclusions from experiments with simple machines and organizes pictures
that demonstrate their principles. Sixth graders, after experimenting,
can explain the principles of simple machines shown in pictures of
nutcrackers, egg beaters, and wheelbarrows. In high school, experi-
mentation also takes place and may be followed by study of pictures.
For example, pictures of the tinsmith's shears and the tailor's shears
enable students to compare and contrast the two and explain their
advantages. Or perhaps, shown a close-up picture of a rowing crew
at work, they may be asked to locate the fulcrum for each lever and
to compare the effort arm with the resistance arm. Diagrams present
a simplified view and help clarify understanding of a complicated
operation—for example, the transformation of petroleum into gaso-
line. Diagrams make effective teaching tools for use in conjunction
with models and mock-ups.

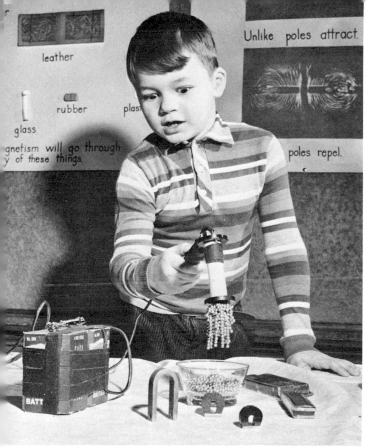

A SECOND-GRADE BOY
DISCOVERS MAGNETISM,
AND WILL UNDERSTAND IT BETTER
THROUGH SUCH PICTURES AS
THOSE ON THE WALL BEHIND HIM.
(PHOTO: READING
(PA.) SCHOOL DISTRICT)

For a topic such as atomic energy, responsible teachers recognize that helping students understand its nature and use is only part of the task. Teachers also direct attention to how atomic energy is related to the aspirations, opportunities, obligations, and general well-being of mankind. One teacher used pictures to show how atomic energy has changed our lives. The class brought in pictures which were grouped under four headings: New Frontiers Opened, Old Frontiers Advanced, Warfare Turned into Threat to Mankind's Survival, and Terrifying Health Hazards Introduced.

Test Materials

True-false and multiple-choice questions do not test a student's ability to apply science in everyday life. The imaginative teacher will use pictures and other graphic materials to evaluate student growth and extension of learning. She will arrange visual presentations of new situations and require students to identify the ideas, processes, or principles involved.

Bulletin boards, chalk trays, desks, tables, and window ledges serve as centers for display of test materials. Each element in the display is numbered so students can place answers on prepared answer sheets, follow accompanying instructions, and move in orderly fashion from one part of the display to another.

One display, arranged for evaluation of the study of weather and climate, contained maps and pictures, accompanied by the question, "Which map would be most helpful in meeting each of the situations presented here?" A picture showed a physician informing a patient, "Your sinus condition is not likely to improve because of the humid weather here in Washington, D.C. Let's locate a better place for you to live." Another picture showed a northern Michigan couple looking at a garden seed catalog. The man was pointing to an illustration, "Notice," he said, "this requires a full ninety days of 70° or more temperature to mature." A third picture displayed an airplane clearly marked, "Crop Dusting—Low Flying." Two pilots were standing nearby, one inquiring of the other, "Do we fly this morning?"

One of several displays to test understanding of electricity consisted of numbered pictures, each portraying everyday situations that require familiarity with the nature and use of electricity. Three of the pictures were a woman and two children under a big oak tree during an electrical storm; a girl placing the batteries incorrectly in a three-battery flashlight; and a man changing a fuse while the switch on the fuse box was turned to *on*. Students were directed to study the pictures, identify the error in each, and briefly explain the correct procedure.

Effective testing can be done by means of opaque projection. A file of evaluation activities to be drawn upon by individual students is still another testing method. This file contains folders with test situations. For example, one folder holds several related pictures along with directions to arrange them in proper sequence. Another contains several pictures, one or more of which do not belong with the others. Here, the problem is to identify those pictures which must be eliminated to make an accompanying statement correct.

SOCIAL STUDIES

Originally, the social studies were introduced into the curriculum as separate subjects, each organized to educate the learner in one aspect of social learning. During the past few decades, much has been discovered about processes of learning and of human growth and development. What we have learned has brought about some changes in the content and pattern of the social studies. In some

THIS THREE-DIMENSIONAL VIEW OF THE UNITED STATES GIVES ADDED
MEANING TO MANY AREAS OF THE SOCIAL STUDIES. (PHOTO: AERO
SERVICE CORP.)

situations it is best to continue teaching social learnings as separate
subjects: civics, economics, geography, history, and sociology. In
other situations social learnings are integrated and taught as a unified
whole and identified variously as the unified studies, core, unit of
study, citizenship, or simply social studies.

Our concern here is not with the organizational pattern for teaching
social studies, but with the role pictures should play in making social
learnings significant to the student so that his imagination is fired and
his thinking is stimulated. Through the social studies, we are concerned with building an understanding of man, his environment, his
achievements, and his increasing dependence upon other groups of
men. Charged with so important a responsibility, it is imperative that
teachers define their teaching purposes as clearly as possible so that
they are able to select pictorial aids well suited to a particular target.

Foreign Cultures

Pictures are helpful for building an understanding of other cultures.
The selection of pictures for this purpose is particularly important.

An injudicious choice can readily lead to half-truths and fallacious conclusions. For example, use in the United States of a picture of an igloo captioned "Eskimo Home" might be as misleading as an Eskimo teacher's use of a trailer captioned "Home in the United States." The unusual has its place, but only among several more representative or typical homes.

Pictures help build understanding of other cultures. For example, pictures of homes in different parts of the world will reveal much about the cultures of the people who live in them. A special niche for display of pictures in a Chinese home indicates the high value of art there, just as the bathroom and kitchen in American homes reveal the importance we place on sanitation.

In the study of a foreign culture, pictures serve to build friendship. Through the Red Cross a teacher may contact a school group in a foreign country for arranging to exchange pictures. The teacher must emphasize the importance of the pictures the class sends, for they will be the materials from which the other school group will form judgments about the United States and its people. Usually, students will recognize their job of communication as an opportunity, a responsibility, and a challenge. They work out plans for screening pictures submitted for exchange, using as the major test whether or not the pictures are representative of American life.

American History

For a topic on our country's development, such as the early pioneers, pictures are part of the unit of study. In the intermediate grades, a picture of a New York family planning to move to the Northwest Territory stirs children's imaginations, if they are made aware of the planning and problems involved in the journey. For example, "What possessions must be taken along?" "What possessions would be taken if there were room?" "Which items must be left behind?"

Once the class becomes interested, the teacher reads sets of pictures with them designed for the teaching of pioneer life—pictures of the journey to the new territory, of a frontier trading post, and of a home. To build a vocabulary, she selects pictures of items such as a blockhouse and a trading post. To carry out project responsibilities, children consult pictures frequently. For example, several pictures of Boonesborough as it looked in the early days are studied in detail by the committee that volunteered to make a model of the town. To make a mural, students use pictures on the preparation for the journey, making trails through the wilderness, and camping at night. Finally, should the group decide to give an original play about the pioneers, a picture file serves as a source so that household chores, recreational activities, and solutions to the pioneer's everyday problems, as well as scenery and stage properties, can be portrayed accurately.

The topic of early pioneers serves as a good introduction to a study of pioneers today. The teacher might ask the class to bring in pictures of the new frontiers of the twentieth century—such as space—that await those who are interested.

Geography

Commercial charts, such as Denoyer-Geppert's "Geographical Terms,"[8] a large, full-color composite that illustrates and names all types of land forms, water formations, and cultural features, are an excellent introduction to map reading, especially when used in combination with maps and pictures. For example, when working to develop the concept of the word *harbor*, the teacher will not be content to use only one chart and one map. She will use a comparative scale to help children fully comprehend that the dot on the small scale map indicates the whole coastal city shown on larger scale maps. She will show views of harbors so that abstract words and symbols take on concrete meaning.

Local Government

Charts are useful for explaining plans of government. In preparation for initiating a unit on plans of city government, for example, a teacher placed on feltboard a build up chart, "The Mayor-Council Plan of Government." On pieces of cardboard of uniform size, simple sketches were drawn and labeled. From strips of sandpaper of uniform width, flow lines were made. The title was placed on the large feltboard and, part by part, the voters, the flow lines, the pictorial representations of the elected official bodies, and sketches of the mayor's appointees. Not only was the chart built up as the discussion progressed, but at a later time students demonstrated their ability to retain knowledge by reconstructing the chart.

In order to carry forward the study of other plans of city government, class committees were formed and each committee assumed

[8] Denoyer-Geppert Co., 5235 Ravenswood Ave., Chicago 40, Ill. "Geographical Terms Map"; 64" x 22," $12.75-$16; 44" x 58," $11-$14.50.

responsibility for making a build-up chart for a given plan. As the students became involved in the process, not only did they become actively interested, but several displayed considerable ingenuity and resourcefulness.

The Community

Students learn civic responsibility by practicing it. In too many schools, community service projects are seasonal, confined usually to Thanksgiving and Christmas. But, in some schools, school service and community service committees help to arrange for and sponsor year-round projects. For example, pictures of the drab rooms of a children's hospital inspired a high-school group to make a series of colored picture panels for the walls. A captioned picture of an invalid staring at the ceiling because he was unable to hold a book led another school group to earn money for ceiling projectors. An illustrated feature story of an orphan child who wanted "a picture of myself" inspired three school camera clubs to make trips to the children's home and the county home for the aged to take photographs.

LEARNING ABOUT URBAN PROBLEMS IN RELATION TO THEIR COMMUNITY, THESE THIRD GRADERS FIND THAT LARGE STUDY PRINTS (ON STIFF BOARD) PROVIDE A FACT-FILLED BACKDROP.

To understand their community, students must be oriented to it. Orientation is easily achieved through visual images of each major part of the community. A school in Parma, Ohio, experimented with a series of 30″ x 40″ air views of the city to teach students about the area in which they live. The project received the enthusiastic approval of students and teachers.

Public Opinion

School should help youth to make intelligent contributions to public opinion. The first step is to make students conscious of how their own opinions are formed. In the social studies class the teacher may introduce the subject by initiating a discussion of some local issue; for example, fluoridation of water. Study would show that a charming woman with lips parted to reveal beautiful teeth was featured in a picture slanted in favor of fluoridation, while one slanted against the measure featured a criminal type pouring "wholesale medication" into the city's water. By following a controversial local issue, identifying pressures at work to mold public opinion, and attempting to secure factual information, students would be challenged to examine their own opinions to see where they stand.

Another step might well be a special study of cartoons, since they are prepared primarily to influence public opinion. Through guided study, students learn to understand the meaning of stereotypes and to note their own biases. Guidance also would point up the cartoonist's use of satire, exaggeration, and caricature to achieve his purpose.

Current Events

Pictures make current events come alive. In a junior high school, a corridor bulletin board became a point of interest when an eighth grade converted it into a current affairs display. News items, pictures, and points on the map (indicated by colored map tacks) were tied together by lengths of yarn. The location of the display and the catchy titles encouraged the entire student body to stop, look, and learn; the well-chosen items effectively arranged for quick comprehension contributed to an awareness that current affairs are everybody's affair.

Twenty selections from cover pictures of *Time* magazine published during a 12-month period were used by a class committee for conducting a "Who's Who Quiz." The pictures were enlarged in an opaque projector; duplicated answer sheets were distributed and directions for their use were given. Participants were required to identify the indi-

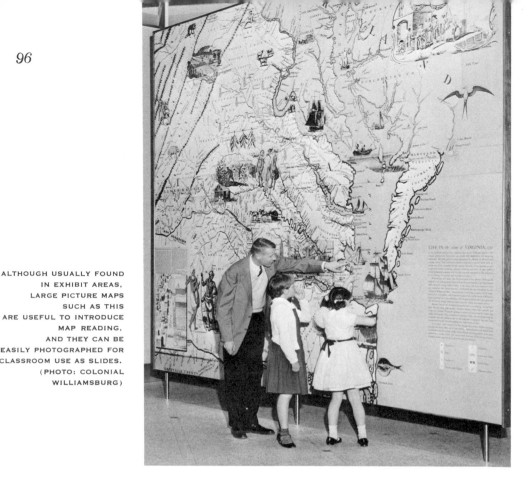

vidual and explain what makes him newsworthy. When the quiz was over, the pictures were shown in the original sequence again, not only as a check but also for an opportunity to learn correct responses through discussion.

In addition to pictures, pictorial graphs are used extensively for current events to vitalize data in newspapers, other periodical literature, and telecasts. It is important, therefore, that young people at every level above the primary grades have guided experience in interpreting messages communicated graphically.

Ability to interpret pictorial graphs is developed readily by students who have opportunity to make their own graphs. In place of the symbolic pictures or isotypes commonly used in commercially constructed pictorial graphs, stick figures and conventionalized pictures can be drawn by young children who wish to make their own pictorial statistics. These same simplified isotypes may be as effectively adapted by more mature students who may wish to introduce a cartoon or other type of picture into a graph.

THE UNIFIED ARTS

For those unfamiliar with integrated arts, the term is used to designate a program in which the content is not divided into fine and industrial arts, but permits plans and purposes to guide learning. This makes it possible for students to design and make projects, moving freely between the two areas of "art" to use whatever facilities or materials are necessary to complete a project. Teachers of fine and industrial arts who have worked under this plan believe that the continuity of experience possible in the integrated program builds an understanding of the relationship among design, function, materials, and processes that is impossible to achieve when the arts are separated.

The teaching of art has been described by Beatrice Burton-Brown as "such education of eye and hand as shall give each individual the power to create for himself some thing of beauty and thus find his own means to express his imagination and emotion . . . the training of eye to see and the mind to understand the visions of artists and the adventures of craftsmen."[9]

Creative Art

Pictures often serve as a stimulus to creative effort. A display of a few wooden puppets combined with pictures showing children attaching the wires to these figures, along with other pictures to show the same children presenting their puppet play, launched one group on a puppet-making venture. Pictures of few pieces of pottery challenged another group to work hard on their own ceramics. The students had never seen such impressive works of the potter's art.

A file of picture materials should be available to help students in their own creative efforts, such as the preparation of a diorama, frieze, or photographic display.

Appreciation of Art

One of the responsibilities of the teacher is to take full advantage of the excellent reproductions of the world's great pictures now available for classroom use. The pictures studied in a school need no longer be limited to whatever reproductions the school possesses. Many American art museums have broadened the base of their services to the community by arranging their treasures to be attractive

---

[9] Burton-Brown, Beatrice. "Visual Aids in the Teaching of Art." *Visual Education* 2: 3; April 1953.

and intelligible to school-age children and by lending some materials to schools (see Primary Source List, p. 125-46). For example, the Cleveland Museum circulates exhibits to schools within a radius of 15 miles, including pictures, photographs, color reproductions, and a limited number of original oils and water colors by contemporary American artists. The Virginia Museum of Fine Arts, in 1953, started an artmobile which toured the state with an exhibit of Dutch and Flemish Renaissance paintings. Many public libraries now offer to home and school the loan of good-quality reproductions of oils and water colors, as well as bound volumes containing excellent illustrations.

The teacher will enlist the cooperation of students in the preparation of a catalog of the pictures on loan or of the originals and reproductions owned by the school. Because the project requires learning about the artist, the circumstances under which the specific picture was done, and the medium in which it was produced, the students become well acquainted with the pictures. Their interest and enthusiasm may even carry over to the entire student body. The completed catalog makes it easy for interested students, parents, and

ALTHOUGH WELL-PLANNED VISITS TO GREAT ART REPOSITORIES ARE IMPORTANT, WHEN POSSIBLE, IT MUST BE KEPT IN MIND THAT EXCELLENT COLOR REPRODUCTIONS OF MOST MASTERPIECES ARE NOW AVAILABLE FOR SCHOOL USE. (PHOTO: CARL PURCELL, NEA)

visitors to the school to learn about the pictures that are placed on display in the building.

Teachers find that pupil response, both intellectual and emotional, is usually improved when an art reproduction is introduced during the study of a cultural epoch or a particular people, or when the students themselves are using the medium in which the artist excelled. Helen Knapp and Abbie V. Strickland[10] have shared with other teachers an account of a fifth grade that learned to appreciate famous painters of the sea. Because the school is located close to the sea where fishing and sailing are commonplace, Winslow Homer's paintings had special interest. As a part of their study of Homer's pictures, the children read poems and songs about the sea. Through reading, they became so well acquainted with the artist that they made sketches of interesting episodes in his life. They went to the seashore to paint. They made scenes of a storm at sea while listening to a recording of "The Storm" from the *William Tell Overture*. Finally, by use of the opaque projector, the class presented at a school assembly a program of Homer's paintings, along with the stories of the pictures. As a part of the program, they told the life story of the painter and illustrated it by original sketches made by class members.

Study of reproductions makes possible comparison between different periods in an artist's work and between members of the same or different schools of art. Study of photographs of art works and illustrations of architecture and sculpture also makes possible detailed study of each subject and comparison between the art of one era and that of another. For example, by studying photographs or photographic illustrations, the student of photography saves time and film. He learns how to find pictures with good composition. He recognizes the perception and skill required to produce pictures that clearly reveal the subject.

Art on Film

After the presentation of a film such as "What Is Modern Art?"[11] where students not only see the color reproductions of painters but also hear excellent discussions of them, several follow-up activities are possible. Teachers might arrange exhibits of reproductions of selected

[10] Knapp, Helen, and Strickland, Abbie V. "Unit of Study of Famous Painters of the Sea." *School Arts* 48: 248-49; March 1949.

[11] *What Is Modern Art?* 20 min., 16mm, sound, color. Riethof Productions, 59 East 79th Street, New York 21, New York, 1948.

A BRIDGE BETWEEN
PERSONAL ACCOMPLISHMENT
AND APPRECIATION,
THE UNIFIED ARTS PROGRAM
DEVELOPS IN STUDENTS
AN UNDERSTANDING OF
THE IMPORTANCE OF
VISUAL COMMUNICATION
IN MANY AREAS OF LIFE.
(PHOTO: CARL PURCELL, NEA)

works of the artists discussed in the film, or the students might be asked to arrange an exhibit, "What We Like in Modern Art," using the reproductions of pictures by the artists in the film. For such an exhibit students exchange ideas among themselves and evaluate some pictures to determine their selections. Such an undertaking permits students to present what they themselves value; they enter wholeheartedly into the project and learn much in the process.

Visual Aids in the Industrial Arts

Study pictures can be an effective teaching aid in the toolroom. While demonstration is the best method for teaching the use of power and hand tools, posters can be effective reminders of proper safety measures and clean-up responsibilities. Production of these posters serves as a challenge and incentive for the development of effective poster-making techniques.

Diagrams showing the correct handling of simple machines are invaluable for students when they check on their own operation of tools. Use of reference charts that show types of saws and hammers enables students to become familiar with the tools and to discriminate among them.

Students may be prepared for a demonstration of a process new to them by seeing an exhibit. Linoleum blockprinting, for example, may be introduced by a display of a wall hanging, a yearbook cover, or Christmas cards—all created by this process. The steps in the process are shown by arranging a series of blocks in various stages of completion, along with the tools used. After viewing the display, students may raise questions which will help create readiness for the demonstration.

In preparation for developing their own designs, the teacher might spend several hours helping students analyze and evaluate pictures of industrial design products and objects of traditional and modern design. Through picture study it would be possible to arrive at generalizations concerning basic differences between a manufactured article and one that is handmade.

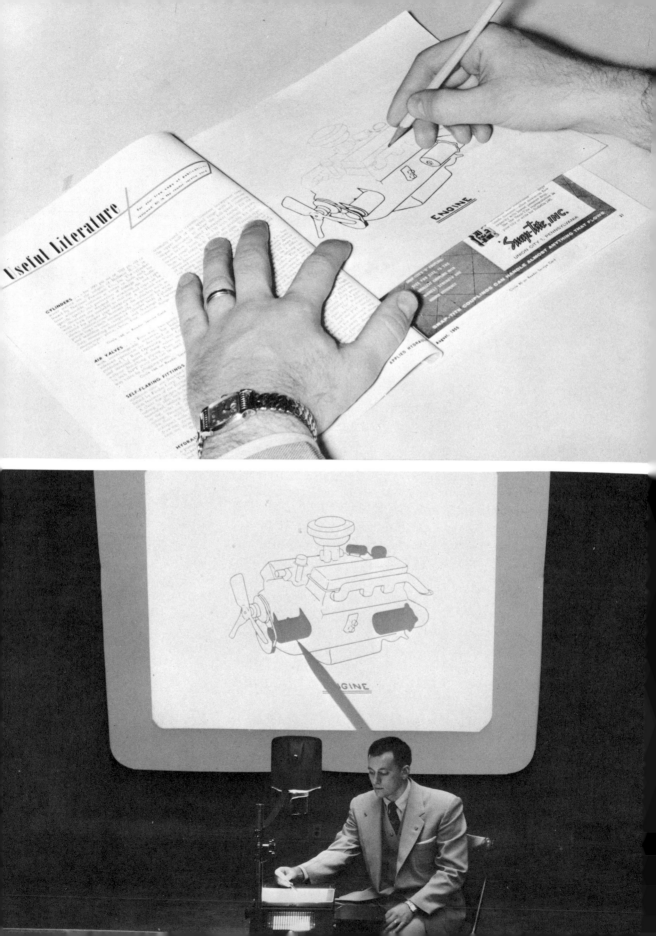

School-Produced Materials

If good picture materials (photographs, illustrations, and pictorial graphs) are available commercially, they should be supplied in sufficient quantities for teachers to work effectively. If picture materials are not available, the problem should be of concern not only to teachers but to audiovisual departments, curriculum specialists, and even school boards. On the basis of production costs, available time, and the school's philosophy of education, a decision must be made on what part the student, the teacher, and the school should play in producing their own picture materials.

The first problem is one of cost. Relatively few school systems have the funds to produce their own teaching pictures. Photographs of study-print size are expensive. Only in large school systems can reproduction of photographs be made at a cost that is not prohibitively expensive. When pictures are produced, they are done under the direction of the audiovisual department, which, in turn, works closely with curriculum specialists and teachers.

Not all school-produced materials, however, are photographs. Work can be done in the classroom if, after weighing the value of teaching without picture materials against the value of spending time producing them, the teacher decides spending time is worthwhile. Before she estimates production time on any material, she should decide if a quick job is sufficient or if the project calls for material permanent and reusable in nature.

The nature and extent of student-produced materials depends in great part on the philosophy of a school. In schools where a high value is placed on the development of attitudes, critical thinking, interests, and appreciation, as well as on the acquisition of information and skills, student production of materials is an integral part of the learning experience. This work provides students with experience in organizing ideas and communicating them to their classmates, their parents, or, in an assembly program, to the entire school. On the other hand, in schools where priority is given to the type of learning that is measurable by response to true-false and multiple-choice questions, students will have little encouragement or incentive for producing picture materials. In these schools such high value is placed on the acquisition of information and skills that other abilities are neglected. Instead of helping the learner discover relationships by increasing his powers of communication through pictorial and verbal expression, these schools provide speed drills and workbook exercises to train him to follow directions and respond to unrelated factual questions.

The following discussion is for teachers and other educators who are interested in investigating the possibilities for producing picture materials and experimenting with production techniques.

PRODUCTION TECHNIQUES

Teacher-Produced Materials

Often, the teacher-produced picture that most effectively aids learning is the hastily made sketch created on the spot to clarify a

TEACHER OR STUDENT-PRODUCED OUTLINE MAPS SUCH AS THIS ONE ARE EASILY MADE ON LARGE SHEETS OF PAPER BY USING THE OPAQUE PROJECTOR.

THERE ARE MANY SHORT CUTS FOR THE TEACHER WHO LACKS SKILL IN SKETCHING OUT HIS IDEAS. (PHOTO: FROM THE BAILEY FILM, ''CHALK AND CHALKBOARDS'')

concept. However, many teachers feel inadequate as visualizers and fail to use this simple method of communication. H. E. Kleinschmidt's *How To Turn Ideas into Pictures*,[1] Marjorie East's *Display for Learning*,[2] or other books that an audiovisual director may recommend, coupled with some imaginative insight, will enable the teacher to develop sufficient confidence and skill to make her sketches a valuable means of communication.

For developing charts,[3] diagrams, and posters, the teacher may wish to trace selected portions from sources which are too small or too complicated for her purposes. For quick tracing and enlarging of a

[1] Kleinschmidt, H. E. *How To Turn Ideas into Pictures*. New York: National Publicity Council, 1950. 31 p.

[2] East, Marjorie. *Display for Learning*. New York: Dryden Press, 1952. 306 p.

[3] Crane, Thomas. *The Teacher Makes His Own Chart*. Columbus: Ohio State University, Bureau of Educational Research and Service, Teaching Aids Laboratory, 1960. 38 p.

picture, she may use a pantograph or an opaque projector. When the opaque projector is used as an aid to production, the material is projected so that the image falls on cardboard or other usable material. The image is traced lightly; later, colored and labeled as required—often by students. On occasion, the tracing may be done so lightly that the outline is visible only to the teacher who uses it as a guide while she develops her picture during the course of the presentation to her class. Frequently this technique is used by television teachers.

Charts and diagrams may be developed on any number of fabrics. Newsprint is useful and economical for a quick sketch. Wrapping paper, brown or white, is an inexpensive working surface. Cardboard, oak tag, chart cloth, and window shading are more expensive, but are durable enough to withstand repeated handling. Chart cloth and window shading can be rolled for storage. When window shading is purchased by the yard or roll, instead of on rollers, individual charts are often mounted on wood doweling.

When a chalkboard stencil of a map or geometric figures is needed, it can be made by tracing the projection on stencil paper and using a leather punch to make the perforations along the traced lines.

For producing graphs, the teacher may purchase stylized picture symbols at office-supply houses, to give the graph a professional appearance and reduce the production time.

Whatever the production problem, the teacher will find the audiovisual director, the art teacher, and the librarian willing to offer advice or to provide reference materials.

Student-Produced Materials

If children are unaccustomed to using pictures as a means of communicating their ideas, they will need suggestion and guidance. The teacher who is inexperienced in helping students plan such materials as murals, dioramas, feltboard presentations, maps, posters, charts, time lines, and pictorial graphs may need orientation before she is able to give guidance. Textbooks and pamphlets in the audiovisual field furnish her with material necessary for helping children communicate their ideas in visual form.

Children should be encouraged to do their work free-hand, instead of taking over someone else's ideas by tracing. Tracing often stifles creative ability and prevents the child from discovering the challenge and joys of self-expression. However, tracing should not be ruled out completely. Often, visual creativity flows from the beginner's feeling

CHILDREN WITH
NO SKILL OR INTEREST
IN DRAWING
CAN OFTEN BE INVOLVED
IN OTHER ASPECTS OF THE
CONSTRUCTION OF DIORAMAS.
(PHOTO: IRENE CYPHER,
NEW YORK UNIVERSITY)

of accomplishment when he traces or uses other visual "starters." And map outlines should always be traced so that they are as exact and accurate as possible.

Lack of facilities and materials need not handicap a teacher who would like to give children experiences in communicating ideas through their own graphic production. Brown wrapping paper and colored chalk are the only materials available to some schools that are carrying forward a program of helping children learn to communicate effectively by visual means. If possible, of course, classrooms should be supplied with materials adequate for children to communicate by visual means, just as they are supplied with pencil, paper, dictionaries, and reference books to learn to communicate by word symbols.

Materials Produced by School Systems

Some school systems have done notable work in producing pictures to meet local needs. The Los Angeles city system is outstanding among them because of its pioneer work and the quality of its productions. The following is an account of the program and methods of the audio-visual section of Los Angeles public schools.[4]

---

[4] This account was submitted, on request, by Margaret W. Divizia, head supervisor, Audio-Visual Section, Los Angeles Public Schools.

Hancock Park is in Los Angeles

Hancock Park is about eight miles from the Civic Center. It takes about twenty minutes to drive from Civic Center to the park. It takes about thirty minutes from the park to the ocean.

Can you find the big streets that are near Hancock Park? Which one runs north and south? Which one runs east and west?

Hancock Park Today

Hancock Park is a county park in the city of Los Angeles. People come to it from near and far away. They see the tar pits as they were thousands of years ago. They look at fossils in the tar. They read the signs that tell about the findings of these fossi Visitors enjoy the beauty of this important place.

In a recent survey, teachers in the Los Angeles city elementary schools were asked to rate the instructional value of several types of audiovisual materials. Films were given top listing, with filmstrips and study prints vying for second place. This enthusiasm for sets of study prints or reference pictures is not of sudden origin. Teachers in our schools have expressed their approval of such material for many years. Until two years ago, all of the picture sets circulated to our schools were produced by the audiovisual section.

Requests to prepare sets of reference pictures come to us from a number of sources. Teachers, principals, and supervisors tell us where basic needs exist. When revisions of or additions to the elementary or secondary courses of study are being planned, a representative from the audiovisual section is a member of the working committee. Audiovisual material which will support the new content is purchased or produced. Often picture sets are a part of the kit of materials. Frequently they cannot be purchased, so they are produced by the audiovisual section.

Since sets of reference pictures (or study prints) have been a part of the instructional materials offered from this section for many years, production procedures have been carefully worked out. For example, in the third grade, children in Los Angeles study about the La Brea tar pits. Except for two good films, a meager amount of audiovisual material on the pits is available commercially. Several years ago teachers asked for a set of reference pictures on the tar pits, so we undertook to produce them.

A talented, imaginative, and successful third-grade teacher was invited to join our staff to prepare the picture set. Following the production routine which has proven so functional, the teacher went to work to develop a set of pictures which would be of real value in a classroom situation.

Planning the set of reference pictures included meeting with the curriculum and audiovisual staff committee to outline purposes and content, doing research on the subject matter, establishing the sequence of content presentation, and checking with a teacher advisory committee to ensure that content met the expressed needs.

Visualizing the content was the next step. It was evident that both photographs and drawings were needed. Our photographers took pictures at Hancock Park where the La Brea pits are located and at the Los Angeles County Museum where animals from the pits are displayed. Drawings were prepared by our illustrators. Historic pictures of early excavations at the pits were obtained from our files and from the community.

The photographs and drawings were arranged in sequence on a story board so that visualization of the content could be seen as a whole. The advisory committee worked with this pictorial presentation to select the pictures which would comprise the finished set and to make any changes in sequence which would further clarify and strengthen the content.

Writing of explanatory notes was begun when all the visuals were assembled and organized. The supporting printed information was written for children to read. In this case the text was written for the third-grade reader. Three or four lines of text were printed at the bottom of the pictures in 18-point Futura Medium type, upper and lower case; the titles were in 18-point Futura Bold, upper and lower case. This type closely resembles type in the books the children use. Identification for the individual set and picture is printed in 10-point Futura Light. Such clear, easy-to-read identification facilitates the work of inspecting the sets that circulate and allows the teacher to put the pictures into proper order quickly.

HERE 700 SETS OF STUDY PRINTS, "SPACE VEHICLES—TODAY AND TO-MORROW," ARE PRESENTED TO SCHOOL OFFICIALS AS A RESULT OF CLOSE SCHOOL-COMMUNITY COOPERATION. (PHOTO: SAN DIEGO (CALIF.) DEPARTMENT OF EDUCATION)

From experience we have learned that primary teachers prefer to have the text on the back of the pictures because frequently they use them to illustrate a chart story which the class and teacher write. Middle-grade and upper-grade teachers prefer the printed information on the front of the pictures.

Designing the set included the physical and technical aspects of production. These decisions must be made when planning is first begun. It was decided to produce these pictures in color, to make them 11" x 14," and to print them on heavy, durable paper stock so that they would withstand handling by children. The face of the pictures was to be coated with lacquer to help keep them clean. The pictures were bled on three sides. The corners were rounded, and a tiny hole was punched about ¾" in from the corner so that the pictures could be pinned onto a bulletin board if the teacher so desired.

Reproducing the pictures may be accomplished in several ways. The audiovisual section of the Los Angeles public schools duplicates pictures photographically or prints them by letterpress or offset lithography. Photographic prints are expensive; they are used when relatively few sets are needed, perhaps 50 to 100. Sets are printed when several hundred copies are to be produced. Printing is the more economical process to use for quantity reproduction. The price of the individual set is reduced as the quantity of sets printed is increased.

To supply picture sets in color has long been a dream of the audiovisual staff. Great changes have come about in the techniques of color printing in the last few years. Now, it is possible to print a limited number of color reproductions without the cost being exorbitant. After some investigation in our community, we found that the pictures of the La Brea tar pits could be printed in color, if 1000 sets were run, for a price which compared favorably with black and white. Since the tar pits will not go out of style and since they are of interest to middle-elementary and upper-elementary grades, 1000 sets would serve the needs of the 430 Los Angeles elementary schools now and leave a few sets to stockpile for the years immediately ahead.

To preserve certain types of pictures for long service, plastic lamination is used. Art reproductions, sets of historical pictures, and natural science materials often are laminated on the machine of the audiovisual section if their size does not exceed 11" x 14." In the case of larger art reproductions, lamination is done commercially.

Packaging the study print sets was done in an assembling room where all audiovisual materials except films are prepared for circu-

STEPS IN PRODUCTION

PLANNING

RESEARCH

WRITING

EDITING

REPRODUCING

PACKAGING

CATALOGING

THE STORY BOARD
IS ONE OF THE STEPS IN PRODUCTION WHICH
FACILITATE PLANNING OF SEQUENCE AND CONTENT

TO INSURE A
QUALITY PRODUCT
DESIGNED FOR CLASS USE,
CAREFUL PLANNING
IS NECESSARY WHEN SETS OF
STUDY PRINTS ARE DESIGNED.

lation. Well in advance of need, heavy seal-rope envelopes were prepared with the set title and the necessary identification numbers. When the pictures were delivered from the printer, they were gathered into sets and were ready for circulation without delay. In nearly 300 elementary schools, there are collections of basic audio-visual materials. Each of these schools receives one copy of all new sets of reference pictures.

Utilizing the La Brea study prints when they reach the classroom takes on great variety. With their teacher, a small group may study the pictorial content, read the informative text, and prepare to present the pictures to the class. Or, the teacher may use some of the pictures to arrange the room environment to stimulate class interest and questions about the pits. As study progresses, the pictures may be placed in the classroom picture file for easy reference.

In the primary grades, teachers are beginning to prepare tape lessons to accompany picture sets so that small groups or individual children may study the pictures and listen to the tape independently when their teacher is working with other children. Teachers are very creative in the way they make use of sets of reference pictures to stimulate, clarify, and enrich learning.

Where To Get Help

We live in a world of pictures. Every day the presses of America flood the mails with pictures. And many of them find their way into the classroom where they are used to improve communication between teachers and children. In our present rapidly changing world, pictures from newspapers, magazines, brochures, and many other sources are prominent in classrooms—a visual bridge between the course of study and the events of today.

MAGAZINES AS PICTURE SOURCES

The alert teacher places himself in a position to know about potentially useful picture material. His interest in significant picture material is multiplied by the number of his students, their parents, friends, and relatives. Some teachers know, for example, that John can and often does bring in recent issues of *Life* magazine and that Fred's father, who is in advertising, is anxious to help when he knows what is needed. Magazines represent a vast potential source of study pictures, and this great picture resource can easily be harnessed for school use by the enthusiastic teacher.

Some magazines, of course, operate special school services that are of real value to teachers. The Primary Source List at the end of this volume provides specific information about several such sources.

BOOKS AS PICTURE SOURCES

Books can be an important source of excellent picture materials—every school librarian has clipped selected pictures from books that are too worn or outdated to be retained on the shelves. Very often, such pictures are important additions to school collections. But, at best, this procedure must be limited to books about to be discarded.

ALTHOUGH PROPER CARE OF BOOKS IS AN IMPORTANT ATTITUDE FOR EVERYONE TO DEVELOP, IT MUST BE REMEMBERED THAT SOME BOOKS CAN ALSO BE USED AS A SOURCE OF STUDY PRINTS. (PHOTO: CARL PURCELL, NEA)

Some schools actually buy an extra copy or two of profusely illustrated books for the purpose of converting them to sets of study prints. When desirable illustrations are printed on both sides of a page, two copies of the book are used to secure a full set of pictures. By cutting the book binding, full-page illustrations are removed intact, ready for mounting.

The content of the curriculum and the extent of the school's library facilities will guide selection of books for cutting. The titles furnished here are cited merely to indicate the excellent study prints, often in full color, which may be secured in this way at a cost no greater and usually less than would be demanded for a comparable set of commercially published study prints, were such prints available.

One book is Joseph Miller's *Arizona Indians*, Hastings House, $1.25, which contains text and 50 full-page, 5½" x 8" portraits of Arizona's Indian tribes—superb informal pictures to help others know the modern American Indian. Since the pictures are printed on both sides of the page, a single copy would yield 25 excellent pictures, at a cost of $.05 each.

America's Wonderlands contains maps, travel information, and 390 full-color 7" x 10¼" illustrations, for $9.95. Another book, *Everyday Life in Ancient Times* (Mesopotamia, Egypt, Greece, and Rome), which is similar in format, contains 356 pages with 120 full-color paintings and many other pictures, for $6. These two pictorial volumes are published by the National Geographic Society. If these books are used for cutting, the cost per color print is less than $.05.

Among the inexpensive books are "Great Americans at a Glance," a set of six, 8½" x 11," heavy paperback books: *Great American Authors; Great American Events; Great American Inventors and Scientists; Great American Statesmen, Explorers, Army and Navy Officers, Historians; Great American Women; Our Presidents at a Glance.* The books are published by Pacific Coast Publishers, Camp-

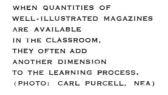

WHEN QUANTITIES OF
WELL-ILLUSTRATED MAGAZINES
ARE AVAILABLE
IN THE CLASSROOM,
THEY OFTEN ADD
ANOTHER DIMENSION
TO THE LEARNING PROCESS.
(PHOTO: CARL PURCELL, NEA)

STUDY PRINTS, FROM WHATEVER SOURCE, REQUIRE A CERTAIN AMOUNT OF HANDLING, MOUNTING, AND "PROCESSING," WHICH OFTEN RE- SULTS IN COOPERATIVE ACTION INVOLVING TEACHERS, LIBRARIANS, AND AUDIOVISUAL SPECIALISTS. (PHOTO: FULTON COUNTY SCHOOLS, ATLANTA, GA.)

bell Avenue at Scott Drive, Menlo Park, California, at $1 each. One book, *Our Presidents at a Glance,* furnishes brief biographical sketches of our presidents, their portraits, and illustrations of highlights of their administrations. The 30-odd illustrated biographies are printed on both sides of the page. For $2, the price of two copies of the book, or approximately $.06 per picture, it is possible to have all illustrations for mounting.

Now that we have noted the actual cost of some pictures secured by cutting picture books, we shall mention a few additional titles to indicate the potentialities that exist when books are considered as a source of study prints:

Burns, William A. *Man and His Tools.* New York: McGraw-Hill Book Co., 1956. 158 p.

Case, Bernard. *The Story of Houses.* Philadelphia: W. B. Saunders Co., 1957. 47 p.

Casman, Frances White. *Fun Around the World.* Pelham, N.Y.: Seahorse Press, 1955. 128 p.

Fisher, James. *Wonderful World of the Sea.* Garden City, N.Y.: Doubleday & Co., 1957. 68 p.

Hogben, Lancelot. *The First Great Inventions*. New York: Chanticleer Press, 1950. 36 p.

Schneider, H., and Schneider, N. *How Big Is Big? From Stars to Atoms*. Chicago: Scott, Foresman & Co., 1950. 40 p.

Tunis, Edwin. *Wheels: A Pictorial History*. Cleveland: World Publishing Co., 1955. 96 p.

Werner, Jane, and others. *Walt Disney's Living Desert*. New York: Simon and Schuster, 1955. 124 p.

PICTURES FROM COLLEAGUES

Since teachers share a mutual concern to make their school an interesting and attractive place, a certain amount of faculty cooperation can be expected in locating and sharing picture sources in the school and in the community. In addition to the centralized picture file in every school building, most teachers will have their own personal collection of pictures. By appreciating and knowing the picture needs of each other, teachers are often of great mutual assistance in building up personal picture files and in strengthening the central picture file of their school. New teachers will benefit greatly from this kind of cooperative picture interest within a faculty.

Leadership, of course, is essential, and in the area of pictures it can be expected from many sources. The teacher who does make effective use of pictures and who is successful in gathering such materials will arouse the interest and envy of colleagues. Much professional improvement is a result of learning from our colleagues. Effective use of effective pictures in a school is apt to spread quickly, provided, of course, it has a sound starting point and is obviously related to the improvement of instruction. Other sources of leadership will be discussed in the remaining pages of this chapter.

LEADERSHIP FROM THE ART DEPARTMENT

Although "teaching" pictures and "art" pictures are viewed all too often as separate and unrelated entities, this should not be the case in our schools where techniques, purposes, and appreciation of graphic arts are developed simultaneously in the child. The graphic arts are a unique language, and a language that must be taught more effectively in our schools. Of course, aesthetics is closely related to all graphic arts, and children stand to gain much if sound aesthetic concepts underlie all picture use in the school.

Properly displayed, well-chosen pictures will do much to make even the most dreary room a more pleasant and attractive environment for learning. At the same time, such pictures can make a positive contribution to what is being taught in any room. Art, like music, invades every area of human activity, and appreciation of the graphic arts cannot be contained in "art appreciation" classes. In fact, it can probably be nurtured best when experienced as an integral part of daily living. Art classes, as such, are important, but art teachers can and should be involved in the broad area of learning from pictures.

Of course, children should be involved in selecting pictures and in determining *where* and *how* they can most effectively be displayed in the classroom and in other areas of the school. This is art in action—students learn important lessons in picture selection and have an opportunity to experience the enjoyment of arranging creatively an effective picture display. An unused corridor, bulletin board, or other display area easily becomes a challenge to students armed only with some pins, paste, construction paper, lettering tools, a bit of imagination, and—most important of all—a rich reservoir of pictures. In this way, as participating consumers of art, students soon develop

SCHOOL AUDIOVISUAL CENTERS OFTEN PROVIDE TEACHERS WITH IMPORTANT SERVICES TO MAKE PICTURES MORE USEFUL. (PHOTO: SAN DIEGO (CALIF.) STATE COLLEGE)

SELECTING AND ARRANGING
PICTURES FOR A PURPOSE
DEVELOPS IN CHILDREN
AN UNDERSTANDING AND
APPRECIATION OF THEIR ROLE
IN COMMUNICATION. (PHOTO:
STANDARD OIL CO., N.J.)

their own standards of what is useful, what is charming, and what is beautiful.

By playing an active role in the school's use and display of pictures (both for art and for informational purposes), students will quickly find themselves in a position of learning not only from the guidance of their classroom teacher but from their art teacher, their fellow students, and, indeed, nearly everyone in the school. For picture displays, regardless of their purpose, attract comments by their very nature: "I like it." "I don't like it." "Why?"

Some easily achieved and important outcomes of this activity will be several obvious but frequently overlooked facts about picture display. First of all, the matter of picture placement will have to be met and students will learn from practical experience that pictures must be displayed so they can easily be seen—at eye level and in a properly lighted area. They will learn also that pictures must be changed frequently enough "to make you look to see what there is this time." Of course, pictures must not be changed so frequently as to deny the opportunity to "live awhile" with a picture. Students may discover that sometimes one learns to like a picture not all at once, but only after living with it long enough to get the impact conveyed through appreciative study of color, line, form, and movement. They may then discover, perhaps, that a bench placed opposite a picture on display in a main corridor encourages those who pass to pause long enough not just to look but to see and feel.

Very often, art teachers will welcome an opportunity to work with a teacher and a class not only in display projects such as those just mentioned but also in the production of pictorial materials for teaching and learning, whether they are teacher-produced or student-produced. The art department will be in a position not only to furnish (or at least recommend) graphic art supplies but also to guide the selection of such items as papers, inks, and paints.

The art teacher is, of course, a specialist who can play a key role with both students and colleagues in raising the school's level of art appreciation and in developing a higher level of picture consciousness throughout the educational community.

COMMUNITY RESOURCES

Every community has many specific sources of useful teaching pictures, such as travel agencies, libraries, commercial artists, photographers, camera clubs, printers, manufacturers, and large retail stores. A first step in tapping such rich community picture resources as these, of course, is for the school to become thoroughly informed regarding the available picture material. Although this can be done at various administrative levels, it will obviously be most effective and productive when it is done on a more personal basis by the classroom teacher or the students themselves. However, for one reason or another, the school frequently does not begin to take full advantage of its community picture resources.

There are several ways to account for this neglect of local picture sources by the schools. School personnel may not have established contacts with local business and industry and, consequently, they are not informed about potentially useful picture material that is, in fact, readily available. On the other hand, the school may have a policy that prohibits the use of business-sponsored materials for classroom instruction. While such a policy does prevent the use of spurious instructional material, at the same time it does eliminate the use of much excellent material that in some cases is by far the best available.

What steps might well be taken so that educationally sound pictorial material concerning local business and industry may be utilized for classroom instruction? The first step may be to revamp school policy. When policy is based on criteria focused on educational values, the school examines all potential resources, no matter what the source, and rejects material of questionable value, no matter who the producer. Such a policy tends to raise the level of materials produced because the criteria become a matter of vital concern to commercial producers as well as to industries which sponsor materials.

Another step is for the school to establish a relationship with local business and industry so that the purposes and needs of the school become well known. When interest is aroused, personnel from business and industry are usually eager to cooperate and anxious to learn ways in which they can contribute.

Many business and industrial concerns maintain a photographic history as well as a file of photographs for advertising and publicity purposes. In one community, the files of a large stone quarry and of a wrecking concern were found to contain photographs which were most valuable for a study of local history. Both establishments permitted the audiovisual director to make selections from the files, and the school was charged only for the prints made from the negatives.

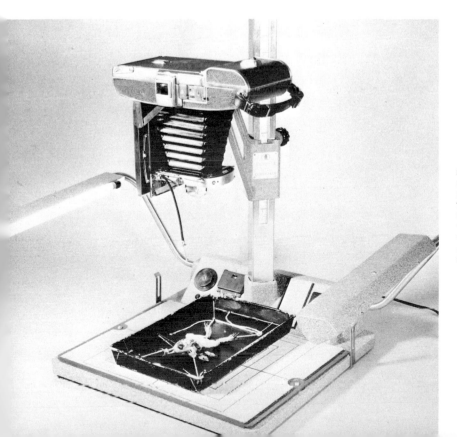

NEW TECHNIQUES AND
NEW DEVICES MAKE IT
INCREASINGLY POSSIBLE
TO CREATE PHOTOGRAPHS
FOR SPECIFIC TEACHING NEEDS.
WHEN SUCH NEEDS ARE MADE KNOWN,
HELP FROM PARENTS
AND OTHER COMMUNITY SOURCES
CAN OFTEN BE FOUND.
(PHOTO: POLAROID CORP.)

PHOTO SHEETS SUCH AS THESE ARE AVAILABLE FROM MANY AGENCIES AND
INDUSTRIES TO INDICATE PHOTOGRAPHIC PRINTS, OFTEN AVAILABLE AT NO
CHARGE.   (PHOTO: UNITED NATIONS)

Parma, Ohio, is one of the many communities in which the school has established desirable working relationships with a variety of local resources.[1]

Following an exchange of visits between the local teachers and the local business and industry, a number of the businessmen invited the curriculum and audiovisual specialists of the school to advise them as to what pictorial materials would be aids to teaching and learning. Selection of materials was made and, in cooperation with the public library, a series of exhibits was planned. Items were exhibited in the main library and several of its branches. These exhibits served several purposes. They made it possible for teachers to acquaint themselves with the materials. They attracted the attention of adults and children in the community and made everyone aware of the public service which business and industry was performing in cooperation with and for the schools.

The library exhibits are but one means of acquainting teachers with new materials available to them through the central audiovisual department. Easily transported, portable displays are arranged and sent out on tours of the school buildings. Teachers appreciate this service, for it helps them readily to evaluate the new in terms of their special needs.

In Parma, professional groups have contributed pictures and other resources to the schools. These groups are often challenged by the opportunity to help orient and educate the children and youth of the community.

The Parent-Teacher Association is another group that works closely with the school to help maintain picture files. And parents perform such services as mounting, labeling, and filing new picture material. Often a member of the audiovisual department or an instructional materials specialist meets with volunteer parent groups to provide guidance and encouragement and to express thanks.

---

[1] Margaret Saylor, supervisor of visual aids and safety, played an important role in bringing about a good relationship with the community in Parma.

Primary Source List
to Producers of Picture Materials

Representative picture material supplied by all organizations listed herein has been examined by the author and in many cases has been used by her students in actual teaching situations. Although all materials on this list have met certain minimal standards of quality and appropriateness, their inclusion here does not constitute an endorsement, per se, by the author or the Department of Audiovisual Instruction of the National Education Association.

It is hoped that this listing of primary sources of instructional picture material will be especially useful to audiovisual directors, instructional materials specialists, librarians, and others responsible for the effective use of such materials in a school or school system. Teachers will find the *Subject Matter Index* which follows this source list a handy device for locating all primary sources of illustrative material dealing with a specific subject area.

Although every effort has been made to make the primary source list (**PSL**) a comprehensive guide to pictorial materials which meet minimum standards, the list is not definitive. Continuing efforts of the Department of Audiovisual Instruction to make this list even more comprehensive are described in the *Preface*, and your participation is invited.

PSL 1   Aero Distributing Co., Inc., 2727 W. Fullerton Ave., Chicago 47, Ill. Over 200 natural-color post card views of Chicago.

PSL 2   Acro Service Corp., Photogrammatic Engineers, 210 E. Courtland St., Philadelphia 20, Pa. Aerial photographs of geographical locations; raised plastic relief maps; vertical prints, 9″ x 9,″ $10-$20; oblique prints, 7″ x 9,″ $1; 8″ x 10,″ $2.50; 11″ x 14,″ $3; no catalog; state needs; special orders filled.

PSL 3   Allied Chemical Corp., 61 Broadway, New York 6, N.Y. Chart on coal-tar products; 36″ x 23″; color.

PSL 4   American Association for the United Nations, 345 E. 45th St., New York 17, N.Y.
>   (a) Posters of flags of the United Nations; 10″ x 15″; $.20 each.
>   (b) Poster exhibit set on good neighbors; $1.50.

PSL 5   American Cancer Society, 521 W. 57th St., New York 19, N.Y. Posters on cancer control; write for listing.

PSL 6   American Classical League Service Bureau, Miami University, Oxford, Ohio.

(a) Study prints on Rome and the Romans; sets, singles; 6½" x 7½"; $.03 each; send for free catalog.

(b) Posters: "Derivation Tree Chart," "The Atomic Age Speaks Latin and Greek," and others; 19" x 25"; $1.50 each.

PSL 7   American Dental Assoc., 222 E. Superior St., Chicago 11, Ill. Chart on tooth care; send for catalog and prices.

PSL 8   American Forest Products Industries, Inc., Public Relations, 1816 N St., N.W., Washington 6, D.C.

(a) Posters on trees, forests, forest conservation; free.

(b) 3 charts: "Growth of the Tree," "Producers of the Tree," "Where We Grow Trees"; 22" x 34"; color; free to teachers.

PSL 9   American Heart Assoc., 44 E. 23rd St., New York 10, N.Y. "Your Heart and How It Works," diagram, 8½" x 11," or chart, 17" x 22"; "Circulatory System," diagram, 8½" x 11," or chart, 22" x 38"; free.

PSL 10   American Iron and Steel Institute, 150 E. 42nd St., New York 17, N.Y. Chart on major steps in steelmaking; 10½" x 24"; free.

PSL 11   American Museum of Natural History, Central Park West at 81st St., New York 24, N.Y.

(a) Range of study print subjects too great for detailed listing; state specifically needs, planned use. Contact prints, 4" x 5," 5" x 7," 8" x 10"; $.50, $.60, $.75, respectively; prices on special orders for photographic work furnished on request.

(b) Charts on man and nature; send for catalog of listings.

PSL 12   American Music Conference, 332 S. Michigan Ave., Chicago 4, Ill. Poster, "Music Is Fun for Everyone"; free.

PSL 13   American Red Cross. Contact your local headquarters. Charts, posters, diagrams on first aid, safety, services, and functions of the Red Cross.

PSL 14   American Seating Co., 9th and Broadway, Grand Rapids, Mich. Posture posters; free.

PSL 15   Artext Prints, Inc., Westport, Conn.

(a) Set of 100 Artext prints, authentic color reproductions organized by grade levels; 7″ x 9″; $40 per set or at special price by grade-level assortments.

(b) Color reproductions published by many art museums; 5″ x 7″ to 8″ x 10″; $.25-$1; send for Bulletin No. 3 (folio prints) or No. 5 (wall-size prints).

PSL 16   Art Institute of Chicago, Michigan Ave. at Adams St., Chicago 3, Ill.

(a) Archives Department. Glossy photos of museum subjects; $1.25 each; matted, $1.50. Color reproductions, $.50 up to $18, depending on size.

(b) Museum Store. Color post cards; $.10 each.

PSL 17   Arthur Barr Productions, 1265 Breese Ave., Pasadena 7, Calif.

(a) Study prints on agriculture, circus, early America, fur trappers, Indians, missions, pony express, rodeo, transportation; 8-30 black and white photos per set, with informative stories; 8″ x 10,″ $6-$22.50 per set; 11″ x 14,″ $8-$30 per set; single photos, $1-$1.25.

(b) Enlarged photo prints, "The Stagecoach" #1 (across the frontier) and "The Stagecoach" #6 (stage-depot activities); 16″ x 20″; $2.50 each. Study prints also available in 16″ x 20″; see study-print listing for prices.

PSL 18   Ash Lawn, Home of James Monroe, Charlottesville, Va. Post card views of Ash Lawn; 6 for $.25.

PSL 19   Association of American Railroads, School and College Service, Transportation Building, Washington 6, D.C.

(a) 40 tinted photographic reproductions with brief explanatory text; 8½″ x 11.″

(b) 3 sets each with 3 charts on railroads in American life for elementary and junior high; 22″ x 34″; color; one set free.

(c) Train display streamer; 8½″ x 160″; color; free.

PSL 20   Audio-Visual Enterprises, P.O. Box 8686, Los Angeles 8, Calif.

(a) *Early Explorers of North America* (1000-1682), 8 study prints in color, with 100 words of study text; on reverse side, black and white drawings with text on the story of the race for land in the New World; $12.50 per set.

(b) *Colonial Living with Paul Revere,* 14 lithograph paintings; comprehensive text; color; $14.50 per set.

(c) *Wild Animals of Pioneer America,* 8 lithograph paintings; drawings and descriptive text on reverse side; color; $9.75 per set.

PSL 21   Automobile Manufacturers Assoc., Educational Services, New Center Building, Detroit 2, Mich. Map of principal materials used in making a motor vehicle and map of United States showing products and trucks used to deliver them; free to teachers.

PSL 22   Bausch and Lomb Optical Co., 635 St. Paul St., Rochester 2, N.Y. Wall chart showing path of light through a microscope; free.

PSL 23   Bicycle Institute of America, 122 E. 42nd St., New York 17, N.Y. Poster on bicycle safety; free.

PSL 24   Boston Museum of Fine Arts, Huntington Ave., Boston 15, Mass.

(a) Photos of objects in the museum, 4″ x 5,″ 5″ x 7,″ 8″ x 10,″ 11″ x 14″; $5.50, $.75, $1, $1.50, respectively; color prints, same sizes, $.25-$5. Catalog, free; handbook, $1.25 plus $.25 postage.

(b) Photos and color reproductions, 15″ x 18″ and 22″ x 28,″ portfolios and sets for loan—limited to New England and New York during school year; free plus transportation costs.

PSL 25   British Information Service, 45 Rockefeller Plaza, New York 20, N.Y. Picture sets, 11 or 12 panels with captions, and photo-posters on life in the United Kingdom and dependent territories; picture sets, $.50; posters, free; list of titles available on request.

PSL 26   Brown and Sharpe Manufacturing Co., Industrial Products Div., Providence 1, R.I. Charts on decimal equivalents and how to read micrometers and verniers; free.

PSL 27   Buescher Band Instrument Co., Elkhart, Ind. Fingering charts for saxophone, cornet, trumpet; 22″ x 34″; $.50 per set.

PSL 28   Buffalo Museum of Science, Humboldt Park, Buffalo 11, N.Y. Post cards of Niagara Falls, birds, butterflies, flowers, Indians.

PSL 29   Chase, Ernest Dudley, Picture Maps, 32 Gray Neck Rd., West Harwich, Mass. Historical and literary maps of many countries; average size, 19″ x 25″; color, sepia, black and ivory; $1 each.

PSL 30   Chicago Natural History Museum, Roosevelt Rd. and Lake Shore Dr., Chicago 5, Ill.

(a) Study pictures of museum subjects: anthropology, botany, geology, zoology; 5″ x 7,″ 8″ x 10,″ 11″ x 14″; $.75, $1, $1.50, respectively; no published listing; state needs.

(b) Set of 12 prints of museum zoological habitat groups; 7½″ x 9″; $.75 per set.

(c) "Map of Mankind" and *Races of Mankind Handbook*. Map—original bronze figures and busts on exhibit at the museum; handbook—geographic locations of races of mankind; informative booklet; both for $1 plus $.15 postage.

(d) Post cards of restorations of ancient landscapes, plants, animals; 3½″ x 5″; 12 for $1.25.

PSL 31   Clay-Adams, Inc., 141 E. 25th St., New York 10, N.Y. Charts on anatomy (human), bacteriology, embryology, first aid; various display sizes; color; $2.25-$18 each, depending on type and mounting.

PSL 32   Cram Co., The George F., 730 E. Washington St., Indianapolis 7, Ind. Complete story of human anatomy presented in 5 life-size charts: "The Muscular and Skeleton System," "The Nervous System and Organs of Sense," "The Thoracic and Abdominal Viscera," "Lymphatic and Digestive Systems," "The Circulatory System"; 7 colors; $86.50, with holder; individual map mounting, $19.75.

PSL 33   Creative Educational Society, Mankato, Minn. (Formerly producers of looseleaf "Visualized Curriculum Series.") All pictures are now in bound volumes, designed to be opened flat for opaque projection.

(a) "Living Together in a Modern World," 8 bound volumes containing more than 900 (8¼″ x 10¾″) documentary photographs grouped under 7 major headings: Vol. 1, *Food* (distribution, health, production, sources, supply); Vol. 2, *Shelter* (builders, building materials, decorating, housing problems); Vol. 3, *Clothing* (climate, culture, fabrics, uses); Vol. 4, *Transportation* (air, land, sea, history); Vol. 5, *Communication* (history, mail, newspaper, printing, radio, radar, telegraph, television); Vol. 6, *Human Resources* (health, education, government); Vol. 7, *Natural Resources* (forests, minerals, soil, wild life); Vol. 8, *Index and Picture Guide*. School and library price, $39.95 per set.

(b) "The Creative Science Series," 4 volumes prepared in cooperation with the American Museum of Natural History, with hundreds of full-page photographs and art illustrations: *Atoms, Energy, and Machines; Earth's Story; Planets, Stars, and Space; The Way of the Weather.* Fundamentals of elementary astronomy, geology, meteorology, chemistry, and physics for elementary and junior-high students; books open flat for use in opaque projector; school and library price, $29.95 per set; volumes sold separately.

(c) "Creative Sports Series," 6 volumes in process of production: *Baseball; Basketball; Football; Golf, Swimming, and Tennis; Recreational Sports; Track and Field.* Write for information.

(d) 7 Julia Greene murals, "Children of Other Lands," "The Circus," "The Farm," "The Home," "Hiawatha," "Mother Goose," "The Old Woman in a Shoe"; 20″ x 28″; color; $1 each; quantity rates.

PSL 34 David Wisner Cenco Educational Films, 1700 Irving Park Rd., Chicago 13, Ill.

(a) Biological sciences: charts on anatomy, biology, botany, physiology, zoology; 24″ x 36,″ 50″ x 40″; color.

(b) Physical sciences: charts on physics, chemistry, atomic weight, basic and advanced periodic tables, spectrum, international metric system; wall-size; color; sold singly or in sets, $4-$12.75 per chart; send for catalog.

PSL 35 Denoyer-Geppert Co., 5235-59 Ravenswood Ave., Chicago 40, Ill.

(a) Over 300 color pictures on American, French, English history; fairy tales; seasons; economic geography; animal life; habitat studies; history of life on earth. Typical size, 29″ x 39″; average price, $3.50 each; send for picture catalog PC56.

(b) Science series, charts designed for elementary and junior high. Group I, *The Science of Living Things:* "Animals," "Animal Classification," "Carbon-Oxygen-Nitrogen Cycle," "Food," "Health and Safety," "Human Circulatory and Digestive Systems," "Human Muscular and Skeletal Systems," "Human Respiratory, Lymphatic, and Endocrine Systems," "Life on Earth," "Plants," "Plant Classification." Group II, *The Science of the Earth:* "Changing Surface of the Earth," "Conservation," "Earth as a Sphere," "Inside the Earth and Layers of Atmosphere," "Maps," "Picture History of the Earth," "Relationships of Earth and Sun," "Rocks and Minerals," "Rocks and Soils," "Time," "Water on Earth," "Wind Systems of the Earth." Group III, *The Science of the Universe:* "Astronomers at Work," "Constellations 1," "Constellations 2," "Depths of Space," "Life in Other Worlds,"

"Meteors and Comets," "Our Moon," "Rockets and Satellites," "The Solar System," "Space," "Space Travel," "Sun and Other Stars." In preparation: Group IV, *The Science of Matter and Energy*, and Group V, *Man's Use of Science*. Each set, 12 charts, 54" x 44"; color; available singly or in sets, in several mountings; paper or muslin editions; see catalog for prices and other sets, including social studies.

(c) Colonial literary-pictorial maps, 64" x 44"; colonial pictorial maps of London, Scotland, England, 50" x 40"; colonial pictorial maps of the United States, 33⅓" x 23"; Miguel Covarrubias mural maps of the Pacific, 38" x 25." All in color; unmounted or mounted; sold singly or in sets; send for price list.

PSL 36 Detroit Institute of Arts, 5200 Woodward Ave., Detroit 2, Mich. Picture packets: *Egypt, Land of Pharaohs, Greece and Rome, Age of Chivalry*; 15 sheets; $.20 each.

PSL 37 Donohue, M. A., and Co., 711 S. Dearborn St., Chicago 5, Ill. 11 picture sets: *Animal Ancestors, Animal Babies, Big Little Animals, Domestic Animals, Wild Animals, Birds at Home, 20 Familiar Birds, Traveling with the Birds, Famous Indian Chiefs, Indians of Yesterday, Wild Flowers*; each set averages 12 pictures; 10" x 12"; color; $1 per set, plus $.25 handling charges.

PSL 38 Educational Research Bureau, 3634 Windom Pl., N.W., Washington 8, D.C. 8 wall charts: "Declaration of Independence" (facsimile); "Flags of American Liberty" in color; "Historical Atlas of Colonial North America"; "Pacific Ocean" (air and army bases), in color. 5 histographs: "Ancient Empires," "Colonial North America," "Pan-American Republics," "Twentieth Century World"; color; $.35 each.

PSL 39 Essex Institute, Publication Dept., Salem, Mass.
   (a) Nathaniel Hawthorne portraits portfolio; $5.
   (b) 9 prints, *Old Time Ships of Salem*; color; $.50 each.
   (c) Post cards of sailing vessels.

PSL 40 Fife-Hamill Memorial Health Center, Health Education Div., 7th and Delancey Sts., Philadelphia 6, Pa. 12 food-value charts; 8½" x 11"; $1.25 per set.

PSL 41 Film Associates of California, Inc., 11014 Santa Monica Blvd., Los Angeles 25, Calif. Set of 15 study prints, *A Newspaper at Work*; elementary through junior high; mounted; 10¾" x 13¾"; $5 per set; reduced rates for quantity orders.

PSL 42   Filmscope, Inc., Box 397, Sierra Madre, Calif. Set of 12 study prints, *Tide Pool,* on animal life in tide pools; teacher text on back of pictures; 11" x 14"; color; $8.95 per set.

PSL 43   Ford Motor Co., Educational Affairs Dept., The American Rd., Dearborn, Mich.

(a) 6 pictures, *History of Measurement;* 16" x 21"; black and white.

(b) Charts on the auto industry; 16" x 22"; free.

PSL 44   Freer Gallery of Art, Smithsonian Institution, Washington 25, D.C.

(a) Color reproductions of 1 American painting, 4 Chinese objects, 2 Indian paintings; $.25 to $1 each.

(b) Photos of objects in the gallery; 8½" x 10," 11" x 14," 11" x 17"; $.75 or $1.50 each.

PSL 45   Friendship Press, 475 Riverside Dr., New York 27, N.Y.

(a) World friends picture albums, 15 pictures per album; black and white; 13" x 10"; accompanying text. *World Friends: At Work and Worship,———At Home,———In Bible Lands Today,———Filipinos, ———In Africa,———Indian Americans,———In Town and Country,——— Japanese,———Long Ago and Now,————Mexicans,———Migrants, ———Spreading the Gospel;* $1.25 per album.

(b) "Picture Books Around the World," 20-page books each with 9 pictures: *Babies Around the World, Children and Their Homes Around the World, Children and Their Pets Around the World, Children and Their Toys Around the World, Children at Bedtime Prayer, Children at Worship Around the World, Children of Africa, Children of India, Children of Japan, Children of North America;* 10" x 13"; color; $1.25 each.

(c) Maps designed to build understanding among peoples; send for list.

PSL 46   General Biological Supply House, Inc., 8200 S. Hope Ave., Chicago 20, Ill.

(a) *Turtox Classroom Charts,* more than 350 subjects on biological sciences; black and white; 17" x 22"; $1 each.

(b) *Turtox Wall Charts;* 30" x 40"; black and white; $3.50 each.

(c) Charts on human anatomy and biological sciences; 30" x 40"; natural color; $12 each.

(d) Charts on Audubon birds and mammals; 30" x 20"; $3.

PSL 47   General Motors Corp., Educational Relations Section, Warren, Mich. 15 charts, some in color, on automobiles, economics, power; 22″ x 34″; free to teachers.

PSL 48   Good Housekeeping Bulletin Service, 57th St. at 8th Ave., New York 19, N.Y. Chart of the history of furniture; free.

PSL 49   Griffith Observatory, Box 27787, Los Feliz Station, Los Angeles 27, Calif. Monthly star maps: Astrorama (star finder), $1; Paloma Observatory, $.95; Zeiss Planetarium, $.50.

PSL 50   Gunter, John W., 1027 S. Claremont St., San Mateo, Calif. Sets of prints, 16 prints per set: *California Indians, Early Hawaii, Explorers of the Southwest, Life in the Wild, Mexico;* 11″ x 14″; color; $15 per set.

PSL 51   Hagstrom Co., 311 Broadway, New York 7, N.Y. Pictorial maps of states of the United States, foreign countries, folklore, literature; various sizes; most maps, $1.50 each.

PSL 52   Hammond, C. S., and Co., Inc., Maplewood, N.J.
(a) Pictorial histories of Britain, picture books for history and English literature classes; illustrations from authentic sources; a brief text accompanies each picture. Titles of books: *Britain's Story Told in Pictures, The Story of Prehistoric and Roman Britain, The Story of Saxon and Norman Britain, The Story of Medieval Britain, The Story of Tudor and Stuart Britain, The Story of Hanoverian and Modern Britain;* 6″ x 8½″; $2.10 per set; $.35 each.
(b) *Je Parle Français,* picture book addressed to beginners and junior high-school students; 8½″ x 11″; $.75.
(c) *Nature Atlas of America,* pictorial library of pets, plants, and animals; $7.50.
(d) *My First World Atlas,* $.45, and *Hammond's Illustrated Atlas for Young People,* $2.95, contain map-reading and comprehension charts, land types, environmental, relief, history maps.
(e) *Hammond's American History Wall Atlas,* history through maps, supplemented by pictorial charts; each double spread 43″ x 29″; $18.95.
(f) Four 3-dimensional anatomical portraitures of the human body: the skeleton and muscles; heart, circulatory system, and muscular systems; digestive and respiratory systems; sensory organs. 12″ x 9″; natural color; unmounted, $7 per set; mounted, $12 per set.

(g) Chart, "Races of Mankind," with a handbook on physical traits, racial stock, migrations, habitats of all races; 32" x 25"; $1.

PSL 53   Hanes, E. G., 2325 20th St., S.W., Akron 4, Ohio. Post card views of Italy.

PSL 54   Henry Whitfield State Historical Museum, Whitfield St., Guilford, Conn. 6 post cards of Connecticut circa 1639; $.29.

PSL 55   Hi-Worth Pictures, P.O. Box 6, Altadena, Calif. Pictures organized into 66 curriculum units, with a story or caption for each picture. Curricular areas: United States, foreign lands, markets, community, transportation, harbors, Indians, missions, pioneer life, American history, lumbering, natural resources, mail, music, animals, farming and farm products; mounted or unmounted; 8" x 10" or 11" x 14"; sold singly or in units; write for catalog and price list.

PSL 56   Holiday Information Service, Holiday Magazine, Independence Square, Philadelphia 5, Pa. Reprints of picture maps: "Animal Kingdom," "Indian Lore," "Migratory Birds," "National Parks," "Evolution Revisited," "Spring Wildflowers"; 17" x 24½"; color; $.10 each.

PSL 57   Ideal School Supply Co., 8312 Birkhoff Ave., Chicago 20, Ill. 6 picture sets on industries: cattle, cotton, fishery, glass, lumber, rubber; 16 pictures to a set; 8½" x 11"; $.70 per set or $4.40 for the entire group.

PSL 58   Informative Classroom Picture Publishers, 31 Ottawa Ave., N.W., Grand Rapids, Mich. Photos: *Life in America* (8 portfolios), *Life in Europe* (10 portfolios), *Life in Other Lands* (10 portfolios), *Social Studies* (15 portfolios), *Story of America* (10 portfolios); 20-48 prints per folio; 9¼" x 12⅜"; accompanying text; $2.95 or $3.95, depending on the number of pictures.

PSL 59   Institute of Makers of Explosives, R. F. Webster, secretary, 250 E. 43rd St., New York 17, N.Y. Safety poster, "Don't Touch Blasting Caps"; with study text; 8½" x 11"; free.

PSL 60   Instructional Productions Co., 2527 Honolulu Ave., Montrose, Calif.

(a) Primary and intermediate sets in curriculum areas: airplane, citrus industry, dairying, farm life, fire department, Indians (Navajo and Pueblo), markets, police department, petroleum industry, transportation, tuna industry, vegetable crops (several sets); 11″ x 14″; $2.50 per set; reduced price on quantity purchases.

(b) Correlated curriculum materials: airplanes, boats and ships, trains, trucks; each with study prints, filmstrip, teacher guide, related materials; 11″ x 14″; color; $25 per set; reduced price on quantity purchases.

PSL 61 International Art Publishing Co., 243 W. Congress St., Detroit 26, Mich. Authentic imported and domestic prints for the study of the history of art; many prints, 11″ x 14,″ $3; others, 17″ x 21,″ $7.50; more expensive pictures in assorted larger sizes.

PSL 62 International Bank for Reconstruction and Development, Office of Public Information, 1818 H St., N.W., Washington 25, D.C. 8 posters, *The Work of the World Bank;* 14¼″ x 20″; black and white; free.

PSL 63 International Communication Foundation, 9033 Wilshire Blvd., Beverly Hills, Calif. Audiovisual kits on Afghanistan, Iran, Pakistan, Turkey, Yugoslavia; each kit: 25-minute sound, color filmstrip with authentic musical background, 1 set of 11″ x 14″ color study prints, exhibit items, illustrated pamphlets. Still photos sold singly or in sets, black and white or color, in several sizes. Also 16 color pictures on each country; 11″ x 14″; $4.95 per set. Write for catalog.

PSL 64 International Labor Office, 917 15th St., N.W., Washington 5, D.C. Posters; free; write for information.

PSL 65 Iroquois Publishing Co., Inc., 1300 Alum Creek Dr., Columbus 6, Ohio.

(a) Set of 16 prints (reprints from textbooks) on American history; color; $1 per set.

(b) "American History Time Line and Date Chart," 8-ft. long wall chart indicating time relationships of important events in American history; color; $2.65.

(c) "World Civilization Time and Date Chart," 5½-ft. long wall chart showing the time span from 4500 B.C. to the present with 5 lines of major cultural developments in code color; $2.65.

PSL 66 Jones, Phillip S., Mathematics Dept., University of Michigan, Ann Arbor, Mich. Chart, "How High-School Mathematics Can Contribute to Your Career"; $.10 each.

PSL 67 Kamps, Norman H. Hand-colored 10″ x 13″ lithograph sets of 12 mounted plates each: *American Pioneer Costumes and Customs,* with text, $22.50; *Costumes and Customs of Mexico,* with text, $22.50; *Aztec Costumes and Customs,* with text, $25; *Mexican Designs,* floral and pictorial; $15. Black and white editions, $4 each.

PSL 68 Kimberly-Clark Corp., Educational Dept., Neenah, Wis.
(a) 6 bulletin-board posters on cold prevention; 14″ x 20″; color; free.
(b) Physiology chart, with teaching guide; free.

PSL 69 Latin American Studio, P.O. Box 3097, Santa Barbara, Calif.
(a) 15 full-color lithograph prints, *California's 14 Historic Flags, 1542-1851;* complete text printed below each print; 16″ x 20″; mounted on heavy card stock; plastic coated; $37.50 net.
(b) 14 full-color lithograph prints, *California's State Emblems, 1849-1957;* complete text below each print; 16″ x 20″; mounted on heavy card stock; plastic coated; $37.50 net.
(c) *Ranch Life in Colonial California, 1784-1846 (Vida Ranchera en California Colonial).* Set 1: 12 full-color lithograph prints, *The Family and the Home (La Familia y la Casa);* English-Spanish titles; text and vocabulary below each print; 20″ x 12″; mounted on heavy card stock; plastic coated; $37.50 net.

PSL 70 Lowman, Hubert A., 3332 N. Corrida Dr., Covina, Calif. Sets of study prints: *California Missions,* 22 prints, grade 4; *Historic Williamsburg* and *Washington, D.C.,* 21 prints each, grade 5 and higher. Sets contain 4-color photos; 11″ x 14″; heavy Kromecote post card stock; satin finish; corners rounded; text under each picture prepared for specific grade level; $10.50 per set, postpaid.

PSL 71 Lutz, Karl F., 537 S. 49th St., Philadelphia 43, Pa. Post cards of Philadelphia and Valley Forge.

PSL 72 Lyon Hobby Mart, Box 63, Hartford 1, Conn. Wide assortment of historic post cards; monthly listings.

PSL 73 Manassas National Battlefield Park, Manassas, Va. Post cards, $.05 each; handbook, $.25 plus $.06 postage.

PSL 74 Merck and Co., Inc., Rahway, N.J. Charts: "Milestones of Chemical Progress," 8½″ x 11," and "Sulfuric Acid Production," 36″ x 23″; color; free.

PSL 75   Metropolitan Museum of Art, 5th Ave. and 82nd St., New York 28, N.Y.

(a) School picture sets on ancient Egypt, ancient Rome, colonial America, medieval life, literature; 6¾" x 3¾"; $.15 per set of 18 pages; 4 sets for $.50.

(b) 4 charts on the relationship between the arts and historical events in the 15th, 16th, 17th, 18th centuries in Europe; $.10 each.

(c) Prints of classical subjects for loan; color or black and white; $2-$20, according to location and type of borrower.

PSL 76   Mount Vernon Ladies Assoc., Mount Vernon, Va. Post cards of Mount Vernon, Virginia.

PSL 77   Museum of the American Indian, Broadway and 155th St., New York 32, N.Y. Pictorial leaflets, photos, pictures of Indians; write for price lists and catalog of publications.

PSL 78   Museum of Modern Art, 11 W. 53rd St., New York 19, N.Y. Post cards of art prints.

PSL 79   Museum of Science and Industry, Jackson Park, Chicago 37, Ill. Color chart, "Tree of Knowledge," 22" x 28"; black and white chart, "When Coal Was Formed," 18" x 28"; send for listing of available charts.

PSL 80   National Audubon Society, 1130 5th Ave., New York 28, N.Y.

(a) Nature charts: animal tracks, bird calendar, bird migration, seeds, trees, etc.; 22" x 14"; black and white; $.25 each.

(b) Post cards of birds, mammals, wild flowers.

PSL 81   National Commission on Safety Education, NEA, 1201 16th St., N.W., Washington 6, D.C. Classroom poster series on bicycles, buses, special days, field trips, fire; 17" x 21½"; $.15 each; single copy free to teachers.

PSL 82   National Confectioners Assoc., 36 S. Wabash Ave., Chicago 3, Ill. Wall-size charts: "Foods Rich in Energy" and "Foods That Candy Is Made Of"; free.

PSL 83   National Cotton Council, Box 9905, Memphis 12, Tenn. Wall-size charts, story of cotton and cotton products; free.

PSL 84   National Dairy Council, 111 N. Canal St., Chicago 6, Ill.

(a) Study pictures on dairy, milk, nutrition; free to teachers living in areas served by Affiliated Dairy Council units or at prices quoted in catalog available from National Dairy Council; send for catalog.

(b) Dairy farm panorama; 40" x 27"; black and white; free, as described above.

(c) Posters and charts on food, nutrition, posture, and health for all grade levels; free, as described above.

PSL 85   National Foot Health Council, P.O. Box 57, Rockland, Mass. Charts on foot structure and foot hygiene; free.

PSL 86   National Forum, 407 S. Dearborn St., Chicago 5, Ill. 6 sets of guidance charts; each set, 33 charts and accompanying book for specific grade group, 7-12; 18" x 24"; $14.85 per set.

PSL 87   National Gallery of Art, Publications Office, Constitution Ave. at 6th St., N.W., Washington 25, D.C.

(a) Reproductions of 29 works of art in the gallery: 24 color reproductions of paintings, 11" x 14"; 5 black and white photos of sculpture, 8" x 10"; comprehensive notes; $6.85 per packet.

(b) 4-color half-tone reproductions printed on heavy paper; $.25 each; send for listing.

(c) Travel exhibits: 10 portraits from the gallery, 10 landscapes from the gallery, 32 color reproductions of paintings and sculpture for classroom exhibit, with information furnished for various grade levels; free plus transportation charges; write for details and information.

PSL 88   National Geographic Society, School Service Div., 16th and M Sts., N.W., Washington 6, D.C.

(a) Color-plate reprints from magazine on art (American old masters), geographic locations, natural history (animals, birds, flowers, etc.), science (atomic energy, chemistry, etc.), and other topics too numerous to list; 48 for $.30, 96 for $.50; write for listing.

(b) Large pictures: mother bear and cubs, wild buck in woods, doe and fawns; sepia; $.50 each.

(c) Color reprints of Newell C. Wyeth's "The Discovery," $1; "Columbus Finds a New World," 16" x 13," $3.

(d) "The Argosy of Geography," graphotint square rigger under full sail; $1.

(e) Charts: "Stratosphere," "Troposphere," "Curvature of the Earth," photographed from "Explorer II" at an altitude of 72,355 ft.; 23" x 14½"; black gravure; $.50.

PSL 89   National Industrial Conference Board, 460 Park Ave., New York 22, N.Y. "Road Maps to Industry," weekly multicolored graphs with facts on current business and economic developments; free to teachers.

PSL 90   Natural Rubber Bureau, 1631 K St., N.W., Washington 6, D.C. Wall-size poster on production and use of natural rubber; free.

PSL 91   National Safety Council, 425 N. Michigan Ave., Chicago, Ill. Safety instruction posters; send for catalog.

PSL 92   National Tuberculosis Assoc., 1790 Broadway, New York 19, N.Y.

(a) Poster, "Protect Them with Shots"; 11″ x 14″; color; free.

(b) School-health posters; 11″ x 17″; color; free.

PSL 93   National Wildlife Federation, 1412 16th St., N.W., Washington 6, D.C.

(a) Set of 4 wildlife art prints, $1; color pictures, 7½″ x 7½″; $.25 each.

(b) 4 sets of post cards: songbirds, western songbirds, wild flowers, mammals; $.50 per set of 12.

PSL 94   Navy, Department of the, Bureau of Naval Personnel, Washington 25, D.C.

(a) Study picture, "How To Display and Respect the Flag of the United States," 18″ x 22″; color; free.

(b) Chart, "These Are the Jobs in the Navy"; 54″ x 40″; color; free.

PSL 95   Netherlands Information Service, 711 3rd Ave., New York 17, N.Y. Set of pictures on the Netherlands; free.

PSL 96   New York Graphic Society, 95 E. Putnam Ave., Greenwich, Conn.

(a) Fine art reproductions 4½″ x 7″ to 9″ x 11″; $.50 per print; minimum order, $2 plus $.25 postage; small print catalog free.

(b) Old and modern masters and religious pictures; master catalog of reproductions published by world's largest art publishers; $20.

(c) "UNESCO World Art Series" in bound volumes; 11″ x 14″; color; available individually; $2 each.

PSL 97   Northwoods Nature and Art Center, P.O. Box 87, Minocqua, Wis.

(a) 7 sets of study prints, animals (ancestors, baby, friendly and wild pets), birds (home and traveling), Indians of yesterday; 10″ x 12″; color; 12 pictures in a set, except 6 in set on Indians; $1 per set.

(b) Hundreds of full-color large study prints from England, France, Sweden, and Denmark; botanical and zoological prints; special list of prints for primary grades; 48 prints from England; 30 New Testament prints from England; 12 New Testament modern art prints; ancient and medieval history; historical and modern transportation; communication; theater. Most sizes 17″ x 21,″ 20″ x 24,″ 30″ x 40.″ Catalogs showing colored miniatures of 120 geography and 120 history pictures available for short-time loan.

PSL 98   Nystrom, A. J., and Co., 3333 Elston Ave., Chicago 18, Ill.

(a) 16 geography pictures, printed on both sides Bristol board; 20″ x 15″; $4.50 per set. 4 pictures each of young rugged mountains, old worn-down mountains, plateaus, interior plains.

(b) *Elementary Science Series*, 160 charts covering 14 major classifications: air and fire (8 charts), conservation (7), electricity (14), geographic terms (5), heat (6), light (8), living things (49), machines (16), magnets (6), matter (4), rocks and minerals (4), universe and space (11); index and teachers guide; printed on both sides of heavy stock in color; 18½″ x 24″; complete series, $90; write for details.

(c) *Fun with the Globe:* 2 sets illustrated self-directing, self-testing cards designed for teaching how to interpret the globe, grades 3-8. Topics covered: continents, day and night, direction, geographic features, latitude, longitude, scale, seasons, transportation routes, vocabulary; $1.65 per set; reduction on quantity orders.

PSL 99   Oestricher's, 1208 6th Ave., New York 36, N.Y.

(a) Large collection of reproductions; color; 96-page catalog and supplements, $1; orders for meeting needs of schools and other institutions receive special care, handling, and rates; inquiries welcome.

(b) 10 uniformly framed pictures to be selected from 100 old masters, moderns, contemporaries; free loan, plus shipping costs; inquiries welcome.

PSL 100   Oil Industry Information Committee. Ask local dealer for address of office serving your state.

(a) Chart, "Petroleum from the Ground to You"; 3′8″ x 2′1.″

(b) 4 charts on the story of petroleum; 22″ x 17.″

PSL 101 Owen Publishing Co., F. A., Dansville, N.Y.

(a) Illustrated resource units: natural science, physical science, living together, world peoples; $.50 each; reduced rates for quantity purchases.

(b) 100 art masterpieces; heavy mat paper; text about picture and artist; 9¾″ x 12¾″; color; write for price list.

(c) "Kindergarten-Primary Arithmetic Concept Charts," 4 sets, 12 charts per set: *Arithmetic Vocabulary* (size, quantity, form, location, etc.), *Measurement Concepts, Number Concepts, Numerical Relations;* 13″ x 16″; heavy stock; 2 colors; $2.50 per set.

(d) "Primary Science Concepts Chart Series," 8 sets, 12 charts per set: *Air and Weather, Animals, Earth, and Sky, Light and Sound, Magnetism and Electricity, Simple Chemistry, Simple Machines;* 13″ x 16″; heavy stock; 2 colors; $2.50 per set.

(e) *Human Body,* 10 charts; 20″ x 28″; color; $15 per set.

(f) *Color Teaching Charts,* 8 charts: primary colors, secondary colors, plus brown and gray; $2.75 per set.

(g) American heritage posters, 3 sets: *Symbols of Democracy, Symbols of Liberty, Symbols of Freedom;* 10″ x 13″; 10 glossy photo reproductions per set; $1.50 per set.

(h) *Community Helpers,* 10 posters of more commonly and less commonly recognized helpers; 13″ x 16″; color; $2 per set.

(i) *Folk and Fairy Tales,* 20 posters of well-known fairy tales; 10″ x 13″; $1.50 per set.

(j) *Good Manners, Good Health, Safety:* 20 illustrations per set; $1.50; reduction on quantity orders.

(k) *Holiday and Special Day Posters,* 20 color posters; 13″ x 17″; $3.

PSL 102 Pan American Union, Photographic Library, 17th St. and Constitution Ave., N.W., Washington 6, D.C. Scenes from member nations and black and white photographic prints for loan; write for information.

PSL 103 Peek, David T., 3845 Guilford Ave., Indianapolis, Ind.

(a) *Life of Lincoln:* 12 reproductions from paintings by Louis Bonhajo; 18″ x 24″; color; school and library price, $18.50 per set.

(b) *The Pageant of a Nation:* 40 full-color reproductions of historical paintings by J. L. G. Ferris, with historical applications by David S. Muzzey; 9½″ x 13½″; mounted on heavy cardboard, 11½″ x 15½″; write for descriptive brochure and price list.

(c) *Book of Antiques for Boys and Girls,* book of illustrations and stories; $3.50.

PSL 104 Pepper, J. W., and Son, Inc., 1425 Vine St., Philadelphia 2, Pa. *RCA Victor Instruments of the Orchestra,* 20 wall charts on heavy cardboard, each chart showing 1 instrument and playing position; 14" x 22"; color; $8 per set for charts and 88-page handbook.

PSL 105 Perry Pictures, Inc., 42 Dartmouth St., Malden 48, Mass.
(a) Study prints on animals, birds, bird eggs and nests, fish, flowers, fruit, insects, plants, marine life, minerals; 7" x 9"; color; $.06 each; minimum order, 20 pictures.
(b) *Trees,* 24 photogravures; 9" x 12"; $1.25.

PSL 106 Pictorial Map Publishing Co., 208 N. Wells St., Chicago 6, Ill. 5 social studies maps in color: "Pictorial North America," 29" x 37," $3; "These United States," 3 maps (history, products and industries, resources), 29½" x 37½," $2.95 each; "Our Pictorial World," 27" x 45," $3.95.

PSL 107 Prothman, Konrad, 2378 Soper Ave., Baldwin, N.Y. Reproductions of famous old and modern paintings, foreign and domestic; size range, 7" x 9" to 30" x 40"; color; $.50 to $20; liberal educational discount; exhibitions of color reproductions are available for making selections.

PSL 108 Publication Services, Inc., 419 New Jersey Ave., S.E., Washington 3, D.C. Decorative wall charts, "U.S.A. at a Glance," a graphic portrayal of the life span and terms of office of every president of the United States, including portraits and great events of each presidential term; 21" x 26"; $1.

PSL 109 Rand McNally Map Co., P.O. Box 7600, Chicago, Ill. *Histomaps: Evolution, Religion, World History;* 21" x 58"; color; paper, $1.50; mounted, more expensive.

PSL 110 Realistic Visual Aids, Box 278, Highland, Calif.
(a) *Across Early America,* set of 24 photos with explanations illustrating the voyage of the "Mayflower," building of the colonies, trails west, and the westward movement; mar-proof ink; heavy poster board; 11" x 14"; $2.98 per set.
(b) *A Big Look at Little Things,* set of close-up photos of ants, bees, etc.; 8½" x 11"; $1.25 per set.
(c) *Early California,* set of 6 photos; 16" x 20"; $1.25 per set.

(d) *The Community, Trains, Ships, Airplanes:* sets of 6 photos each; 16″ x 19″; black and white; $1.25 per set.

PSL 111 San Francisco Museum of Art, Civic Center, San Francisco 2, Calif.

(a) Sets of art reproductions, 12 in each set: *Latin American Collection, Mexican Collection, Museum Collection;* in folder with leaflet; 9½″ x 10″; black and white; $.30 per set.

(b) Museum color reproductions; $.50 each.

(c) Post cards of works of graphic arts.

PSL 112 Schmitt, Hall and McCreary, Park Ave. at 6th St., Minneapolis 15, Minn.

(a) 2 sets, 20 duotone etchings each, *Portraits of Great Composers;* 7¾″ x 9″; portfolio edition, $1.75; bound portfolio, $2; write for list of composers.

(b) Historical panorama wall chart; wooden edges; hanging loop; 36″ x 48″; color; $4.50; student edition, 17″ x 22,″ $.75.

PSL 113 Scott, Foresman and Co., 433 E. Erie St., Chicago 11, Ill.

(a) *Science Is Wondering:* 16 charts; printed back to back on heavy cardboard; 20″ x 25″; color; organized for kindergarten on problems dealing with pets, plants, sounds, wheels; $7.60 per set.

(b) *The Kindergarten Health and Safety Pictures:* 16 charts; printed on sturdy cardboard; 16″ x 19″; color; $7.60 per set.

(c) The following 20″ x 27″ charts are available free when ordered by number: "Are You Smart About Safety at School?" (#241), "Bulletin Board Lessons for First Graders" (#654), "Bulletin Board Lessons on Phonetic Skills for 2nd and 3rd Grade" (#656), "Choosing a Good Breakfast" (#630), "Energy Chart" (#702), "Getting Work Done" (#251), "Growing Up Physically" (#518), "How Do Heating and Cooling Change Materials?" (#221), "In All Our States" (#781), "Let's Drive Right" (#710), "Know Your Dictionary—Say the Word Chart" (#769), "Let's Play Checkroom" (#426), "Let's Talk About Dogs" (#777), "Maps of Spain and South America" (#445), "Make the Most of Your Dictionary" (#308), "Number Line Chart" (#682), "Office Holders Chart" (#516), "Skeleton Teaching Kit" (#746), "When We Sleep" (#646).

PSL 114 Scripta Mathematica, Yeshiva University, New York 33, N.Y. Post cards of geometric forms, mathematicians, mathematics, scientists; 6½″ x 9½,″ 7″ x 15″; sold singly, $.10-$.50, and in sets.

PSL 115   Society for Visual Education, 1345 Diversey Parkway, Chicago 14, Ill. 121 art reproduction prints on heavy paper suitable for framing; 18½" x 23½," 20½" x 26"; color; $2.95 each; minimum order of 3 prints; send for listing.

PSL 116   Soil Conservation Service, Information Division, U.S. Dept. of Agriculture, Washington 25, D.C. Soil conservation poster charts; single copy free.

PSL 117   Sonotone Corp., Professional Relations Dept., Elmsford, N.Y. Chart: "How We Hear," 8½" x 11" or 26" x 36"; "Diagram of Human Ear," 8½" x 11" or 26" x 33"; free.

PSL 118   Southwest Museum, Box 128, Highland Park, Los Angeles 42, Calif. Study picture, "Typical Indian Dwellings of the United States"; 16" x 19"; $.35; write for catalog.

PSL 119   Sportsmen's Service Bureau, 250 E. 43rd St., New York 17, N.Y. 6 posters on gun safety; color; free set to a school; additional set, $.25.

PSL 120   Superintendent of Documents, Government Printing Office, Washington 25, D.C. Send for Catalog PL 81.
(a) Charts on agriculture, industrial safety, nutrition, weather, etc.; $.05-$1.25.
(b) Posters on armed forces, Bill of Rights, food, etc.; $.05-$1.

PSL 121   Teaching Film Custodians, Inc., 25 W. 43rd St., New York 36, N.Y. 10-12 glossy prints in sets on drama, history, literature, speech, social studies; 8" x 10"; $3 per set to schools, colleges, libraries; send for listing.

PSL 122   Tennessee Valley Authority, Information Office, Knoxville, Tenn. Chart of major dams of TVA area and facts about them; 17" x 11"; free.

PSL 123   United Air Lines, School and College Service, 5959 S. Cicero Ave., Chicago 38, Ill.
(a) 2 sets of 16 pictures each: *History of the Mail* and *Historic Planes;* 8½" x 11"; free.
(b) Chart, "Air Cargo Today"; 22" x 33"; free.

PSL 124   United Fruit Co., Educational Service Dept., Pier 3, North River, New York 6, N.Y. Wall chart, "Bananaland," with pictorial leaflet; state maturity level to be served; color; free to teachers.

PSL 125 United Nations, Public Inquiries Unit, Dept. of Public Information, New York, N.Y., for free materials. International Documents Service, Columbia University Press, 2960 Broadway, New York 27, N.Y., for other materials. Write for information.

(a) Set of 16 photographic posters on activities of the United Nations; 14" x 20"; black and white; $1.25.

(b) UN flag chart; 18" x 14"; color; $.15.

(c) Chart, "Organs of the United Nations"; 21" x 15"; single copy free to teachers.

(d) Set of 8 posters, *For the Children,* on the work of UNICEF; 14" x 20"; $1 per set.

(e) Set of 4 posters of the Universal Declaration of Human Rights; 30" x 40"; color; $.50.

(f) "Student Map of the United Nations"; 28" x 22"; $.15.

PSL 126 United States Beet Sugar Assoc., Tower Building, Washington 5, D.C. Wall charts included in teaching kit on beet sugar; color; free.

PSL 127 United States Committee for the UN, 375 Park Ave., New York 22, N.Y. UN posters; free; send for illustrated booklet.

PSL 128 United States Library of Congress, Information and Publications Office, Washington 25, D.C.

(a) Historical documents and photographs reproduced by the photoduplication service of the library; minimum order charge, $1.50. Examples: "Declaration of Independence" (photostat), $.90; "Mayflower Compact" (photostat), $.55; "Signers of the Constitution" (photostat), $.90.

(b) "Captain John Smith's Map of Virginia" (facsimile), with brochure; $1.75 from card division of library.

(c) *Pictorial Americana,* a list of photographic negatives in the prints and photographs division of the library; $.25.

PSL 129 United States Steel Corp., 71 Broadway, Room 1800, New York 6, N.Y.

(a) 22 captioned study prints and teachers manual on steelmaking, available separately or as a part of a kit which includes wall chart and color filmstrip; 8½" x 11"; black and white; 1 kit per teacher; free.

(b) Chart, "How Steel Is Made"; 35" x 45"; color; linen back; free.

PSL 130 Upjohn Co., Trade and Guest Relations Dept., 301 Henrietta St., Kalamazoo, Mich. Reprints from Norman Rockwell's paintings, 8 color plates of discoverers from fields of medicine and pharmacy, 6 color plates of family and family doctor; 15½" x 19"; free.

PSL 131 Venus Pen and Pencil Corp., Lewisburg, Tenn. Wall chart, "Story of the Lead Pencil"; free.

PSL 132 Walters Art Gallery, 600 N. Charles St., Baltimore 1, Md. Post cards; see catalog.

PSL 133 Ward's Natural Science Establishment, Inc., P.O. Box 1712, Rochester 3, N.Y. Anatomical wall charts useful for biology, first aid, physical education, and science; life size or greatly enlarged; average size, 44" x 35"; some charts black and white, some color; sold singly or in sets; many priced around $8.

PSL 134 Wedberg and Associates, Box 62, West Covina, Calif. 14 study prints on community bakery, with short descriptions; for primary grades; plastic coated; $4 per set.

PSL 135 W. M. Welch Scientific Co., Div. of W. M. Welch Mfg. Co., 1515 Sedgwick St., Chicago 10, Ill.

(a) 7 aeronautics charts; 42" x 58"; color; $25.25.

(b) 4 Audubon bird charts: "Summer Birds," "Winter Birds," "Game Birds," and "Birds of Prey"; 20" x 30"; color; $3.

(c) 4 mammal and bird charts; 20" x 30"; color; $3.

(d) 30 diagrammatic botanical charts; 24" x 36"; color; $27.50.

(e) 40 general science charts; for elementary and junior high; 29" x 42"; color; $42.50.

(f) 12 health charts; for elementary grades; 29" x 42"; color; $18.

(g) 60 physics charts; for high school and junior college; 29" x 42"; color; $60.

(h) 30 physiology, health, hygiene charts; 29" x 42"; color; lithographed on heavy paper; $37.50.

(i) 30 diagrammatic zoological charts; 24" x 36"; color; $27.50.

PSL 136 Wild Flower Preservation Society, Inc., 3740 Oliver St., N.W., Washington 15, D.C. Post cards; send for listing.

PSL 137 Wilson Sporting Goods Co., 2233 West St., River Grove, Ill. Chart, "Field and Court Dimensions"; 18" x 22"; free.

PSL 138 Woman's Day, Inc., 67 W. 44th St., New York 36, N.Y. Chart, "Presidents of the United States"; 25¾" x 34¾"; folded, $.50; tube mailer, $.65.

Subject Index
to Primary Source List

Producers of picture materials included in the *Primary Source List* (PSL) on the preceding pages will, in most cases, have pictures covering many subject areas. As a guide to this material, the following comprehensive *Subject Index* has been prepared. It is intended to assist the teacher who has a specific need for picture material. A key to the letters in parenthesis following the PSL number follows:

A—Assorted audiovisual media
C—Chart
D—Diagram
F—Facsimile
G—Graph
H—Histograph
M—Map
Mu—Mural

P { Art reproduction print / Picture / Print / Study print
PC—Post card
Ph—Photograph
Po—Poster

A

Abdominal and thoracic viscera, human, PSL 32 (C)
Aerial photographs, PSL 2
Aeronautical charts, PSL 135a
Afghanistan, PSL 63 (A)
Africa
  Children of, PSL 45b (P)
  World friends, PSL 45a (P)
Age of chivalry, PSL 36 (P)
Agriculture, PSL 17a (A); PSL 120a (C) (*see also* Farms; Foods)
Air, elementary science, PSL 98b (C); PSL 101d (C)
Air cargo today, PSL 123b (C)
Airplanes, PSL 33a (Ph); PSL 60a (P); b (A); PSL 110d (Ph) (*see also* Transportation)
  Aerial photographs, PSL 2
  Aeronautical charts, PSL 135a
  Air cargo today, PSL 123b (C)
  Historic, PSL 123a (P)
American heritage, PSL 101g (Po)
American history. See United States *under* History.
American life, PSL 58 (Ph) (*see also* United States)

American Life (Cont'd.)
  Colonial days, PSL 20b (P); PSL 35c (M); PSL 38 (C); PSL 75a (P); PSL 110a (Ph)
  Early times, PSL 17a (A); PSL 110a (Ph)
  Living together in modern world, PSL 33a (Ph)
  Pictorial Americana, PSL 128c (Ph)
  Pioneer America, wild animals of, PSL 20c (P)
  Westward movement, PSL 110a (Ph)
American Red Cross, services and functions of, PSL 13 (A)
Anatomy, human, PSL 31 (C); PSL 32 (C); PSL 34a (C); PSL 46c (C); PSL 52f (P); PSL 101e (C), PSL 133 (C) (*see also* Physiology)
Ancient empires, PSL 38 (H)
Animals, PSL 33a (Ph); PSL 35a (P), b (C); PSL 37 (P); PSL 52c (P); PSL 55 (P); PSL 88a (P); PSL 105a (P) (*see also* Pets)
  Ancestors, PSL 37 (P), PSL 97a (P)

Selected References

PRODUCTION, PROCESSING, AND DISPLAY OF PICTURE MATERIALS

Books and Periodicals

ALEXANDER, M. E. "Preparing and Filing Mounted Materials." *National Elementary Principal* 13: 194-98; June 1934.

CRANE, THOMAS. *The Teacher Makes His Own Charts.* Columbus: The Ohio State University, Bureau of Educational Research and Service, Teaching Aids Laboratory, 1960. 38 p.

DENT, CHARLES HERGER, and TIEMANN, E. F. *Bulletin Boards for Teaching.* Austin: University of Texas, Visual Instruction Bureau, 1958. 38 p.

DENT, CHARLES HERGER, and OTHERS. *Tear Sheets for Teaching.* Austin: University of Texas, Visual Instruction Bureau, 1954. 24 p.

EAST, MARJORIE. *Display for Learning.* New York: Dryden Press, 1952. 306 p.

EAST, MARJORIE. "Try a 3-D Bulletin Board." *Instructional Materials* 1: 68; May 1956.

FOSTER, I. R. "Care and Filing of Pictures." *International Journal of Religious Education* 29: 16-18; May 1953.

FRYE, H. R. "Preparation of Inexpensive Visual Materials." *Educational Screen and Audio-Visual Guide* 35: 216-17; June 1956.

GIBSON, JAMES J. "A Theory of Pictorial Perception." *Audio-Visual Communication Review* 2: 3-23; Winter 1954.

GRASSELL, E. MILTON. "Simplicity Sets Tone for Bulletin Board Displays." *Instructional Materials* 1: 106-107; June 1956.

HAAS, KENNETH, and PACKER, HARRY. *Preparation and Use of Visual Aids.* New York: Prentice-Hall, 1946. 224 p.

IRELAND N. O. *Picture File in Schools, Colleges, and Public Libraries.* Boston: F. W. Faxon Co., 1952. 136 p.

KELLY, MARJORIE, and RONKES, NICHOLAS. *Matting and Displaying the Work of Children.* San Francisco: Fearon Publishers, 1957. 32 p.

KINDER, JAMES S. *Audio-Visual Materials and Techniques.* New York: American Book Co., 1950. 624 p.

KOSKEY, THOMAS. *Baited Bulletin Boards.* San Francisco: Fearon Publishers, 1954. 32 p.

LIECHTI, ALICE O., and CHAPPELL, JACK R. *Making and Using Charts.* San Francisco: Fearon Publishers, 1957. 56 p.

MEEKS, MARTHA F. *Lettering Techniques.* Austin: University of Texas, Visual Instruction Bureau, 1956. 33 p.

MICH, DANIEL D., and EBERMAN, EDWIN. *Technique of the Picture Story.* New York: McGraw-Hill Book Co., 1945. 239 p.

MILES, K. B. "Visual Aids with Your Box Camera." *School Arts* 55: 10-22; October 1955.

MILLER, BRUCE. *So You Want To Start a Picture File*. Riverside, Calif.: the Author (Box 369), 1956. 35 p.

MORELAND, H. E. "Manipulated Mounting Develops Work Experience." *Audio-Visual Guide* 20: 13-14; January 1954.

MUSEUM OF MODERN ART. *How To Take Care of Your Pictures*. New York: the Museum, 1954. 54 p.

NICHOLS, V. R. "Dry Mount Technique." *Educational Screen and Audio-Visual Guide* 37: 22; January 1958.

OHIO STATE UNIVERSITY, THE. *How To Keep Your Bulletin Board Alive*. Columbus: the University, Bureau of Educational Research and Service, Teaching Aids Laboratory, 1958. 15 p.

OLSON, ROBERT H. "Make a Three-Way Display for Learning." *Teaching Tools* 3: 132-33; Summer 1956.

RAY, HENRY W. "Using the Inexpensive Camera." *Audio-Visual Instruction* 2: 174-75; June 1957.

RUFSVOLD, M. I. *Audio-Visual School Library Service; A Handbook for Librarians*. Chicago: American Library Association, 1949. 116 p.

SALEN, G. P. "Stick 'Em Up!" *Educational Screen and Audio-Visual Guide* 37: 76-77; February 1958.

SALISBURY, GORDON S. "Sponsored Materials—Lesson in Filing." *Audio-Visual Instruction* 1: 219; December 1956.

SMITH, ETHEL BEATTY. "Let a Camera Help You Teach." *Business Education World* 30: 223-25; January 1950.

WEAVER, GILBERT, and BOLLINGER, ELROY W. *Visual Aids: Their Construction and Use*. New York: D. Van Nostrand Co., 1949. 388 p.

WILSON, ROBERT R. "Photography: A New Educational Tool." *Audio-Visual Instruction* 2: 172-74; June 1957.

WITTICH, WALTER, and SCHULLER, CHARLES. *Audio-Visual Materials; Their Nature and Use*. New York: Harper & Brothers, 1953. 564 p.

Films and Filmstrips

Better Bulletin Boards. 13 min., 16mm, sound, color and b & w. Audio-Visual Center, Bloomington, Indiana, 1956.

Bulletin Boards, An Effective Teaching Device. 11 min., 16mm, sound, color. Bailey Films, 6509 De Longpre Avenue, Hollywood 28, California, 1956.

Creating Cartoons. 10 min., 16mm, sound, b & w. Bailey Films, 6509 De Longpre Avenue, Hollywood 28, California, 1955.

How To Keep Your Bulletin Board Alive. 33 frames, color. The Ohio State University, Bureau of Educational Research and Service, Teaching Aids Laboratory, Columbus 10, Ohio, 1950.

How To Make a Picture Frame. 21 frames, b & w. Visual Educational Consultants, 2066 Helena Street, Madison 4, Wisconsin, 1956.

Mounting Pictures. 52 frames, color. University of Texas, Visual Instruction Bureau, Austin 12, Texas, 1956.

Parade of Bulletin Boards. 45 frames, color. The Ohio State University, Bureau of Educational Research and Service, Teaching Aids Laboratory, Columbus 10, Ohio, 1957.

Passe Partout Framing. 10 min., 16mm, sound, color and b & w. Indiana University, Bloomington, Indiana, 1956.

Successful Exhibit Ideas. 81 frames, b & w. National Publicity Council, 257 Fourth Avenue, New York 10, New York, 1958.

This Is Color. 27 min., 16mm, sound, color. Modern Talking Picture Service, 3 East 54th Street, New York 22, New York, 1957.

Wet Mounting Pictorial Materials. 11 min., 16mm, sound, color and b & w. Indiana University, Bloomington, Indiana, 1952.

SELECTION AND UTILIZATION OF PICTURE MATERIALS

Books and Periodicals

AMERICAN ASSOCIATION OF SCHOOL ADMINISTRATORS. *Choosing Free Materials for Use in the Schools.* Washington, D.C.: the Association, a department of the National Education Association, 1955. 24 p.

AMMONS, R. B., and MANAHAN N. "Full-Range Picture Vocabulary Test." *Journal of Educational Research* 44: 14-21; September 1950.

ASSOCIATION FOR SUPERVISION AND CURRICULUM DEVELOPMENT. *Using Free Materials in the Classroom.* Washington, D.C.: the Association, a department of the National Education Association, 1953. 16 p.

BLANC, S. S. "Selecting and Using Flat Pictures and Stereographs." *Audio-Visual Guide* 19: 49-50; October 1952.

BLOSS, E. L. "Focus on Flats." *Instructor* 64: 12; March 1955.

BROCKMYER, I. "Testing with Pictures." *Journal of Geography* 50. 54-57; February 1951.

BUSWELL, GUY T. *How People Look at Pictures.* Chicago: University of Chicago Press, 1935. 198 p.

CHANDLER, ANNA CURTIS, and CYPHER, IRENE F. *Audio-Visual Techniques for Enrichment of the Curriculum.* New York: Noble and Noble, 1948. 252 p.

COLLINS, L. "Postcards for Visual Education." *Hobbies* 56: 1-150; September 1951.

DALE, EDGAR. *Audio-Visual Methods in Teaching.* Revised edition. New York: Dryden Press, 1954. 534 p.

DALE, EDGAR. "Seeing the Meaning." *Educational Screen* 27: 11-12; January 1948.

DE KIEFFER, ROBERT, and COCHRAN, LEE W. *Manual of Audio-Visual Techniques.* New York: Prentice-Hall, 1955. 220 p.

DIETRICH, GRACE L., and HUNNICUT, C. W. "Art Content Preferred by Primary-Grade Children." *Elementary School Journal* 48: 557-59; June 1948.

DENT, ELLSWORTH, C. *Audio-Visual Handbook.* Sixth revised edition. Chicago: Society for Visual Education, 1949. 220 p.

EMERY, J. N. "Pictures; Low-Cost Visual Aid." *Grade Teacher* 67: 94-95; September 1949.

FRAZIER, ALEXANDER, and RAYMOND, JOHN C. "Reading Pictures; Report of a Unit." *English Journal* 37: 394-99; October 1948.

FRENCH, JOHN E. "Children's Preferences for Pictures of Varied Complexity of Pictorial Pattern." *Elementary School Journal* 53: 90-95; October 1952.

GANTT, MILDRED MYRTLE. "Picture Selection for the Secondary School Library." *Wilson Library Bulletin* 21: 428-30; February 1947.

GIBSON, JAMES J. *The Perception of the Visual World.* Boston: Houghton Mifflin Co., 1950. 235 p.

GIBSON, JAMES J. "A Theory of Pictorial Perception." *Audio-Visual Communication Review* 2: 3-23; Winter 1954.

GREEN, IVAH. "Blow It Up with the Opaque Projector." *Teaching Tools* 5: 22-23; Winter 1958.

GREEN, IVAH. "Show Us a Picture." *Teaching Tools* 2: 22-25; Fall 1954.

HICKS, WILSON. *Words and Pictures.* New York: Harper & Brothers, 1952. 171 p.

HOBAN, C. F.; HOBAN, C. F., JR.; and ZISMAN, S. B. *Visualizing the Curriculum.* New York: Cordon Co., 1937. 300 p.

KINDER, JAMES S. *Audio-Visual Materials and Techniques.* New York: American Book Co., 1950. 624 p.

LEMOS, JOHN T. *Planning and Producing Posters.* Worcester, Mass.: Davis Press, 1947. 60 p.

LOCKRIDGE, J. PRESTON. "Flexible and Inexpensive." *Audio-Visual Instruction* 2: 266-67; December 1957.

LOGAN, MARGUERITE. "Pictures as Geographic Tools." *NEA Journal* 39: 44-46; January 1950.

McKOWN, HARRY C., and ROBERTS, ALBIN B. *Audio-Visual Aids to Instruction.* Second edition. New York: McGraw-Hill Book Co., 1949. 608 p.

MARCH, LELAND S. "Social Learning Through Pictures." *Audio-Visual Materials and Methods in the Social Studies.* Eighteenth Yearbook. Washington, D.C.: National Council for the Social Studies, National Education Association, 1947. Chapter 9, p. 83-87.

MICHAELIS, JOHN L. *Social Studies and Children in a Democracy.* New York: Prentice-Hall, 1950. 466 p.

MORGAN, HENRY H. "Measuring Achievement Motivation with Picture Motivations." *Journal of Consulting Psychology* 17: 287-92; August 1953.

PARKER, EDITH PUTNAM. "Pictures as Laboratory Materials in Geography." *Education* 64: 434-47; March 1944.

PRICE, L. "Enriching Our Curriculum Through Picture Study." *Journal of Education* 36: 105-106; January 1954.

RAYMOND, J. C., and FRAZIER, A. "Reading Pictures." *English Journal* 37: 394-99; October 1948.

RESS, ETTA S. *Use of Pictures To Enrich School Resources.* Mankato, Minn.: Creative Education Society, 1953. 32 p.

ROSENTHAL, HERBERT C. "Graphics for Vivid Communication." *Audio-Visual Instruction* 1: 216-17; December 1956.

RUDISILL, MABEL F. "Children's Preferences for Color Versus Other Qualities in Illustrations." *Elementary School Journal* 52: 444-51; April 1952.

SANBORN, WILLIAM B. "San Francisco's Audio-Visual Materials Catalog." *Educational Screen and Audio-Visual Guide* 37: 384-85; August 1958.

SANDS, LESTER B. *Audio-Visual Procedures in Teaching.* New York: Ronald Press Co., 1956. 670 p.

SANDS, LESTER B. "Teaching with Pictures." *Grade Teacher* 74: 55; October 1956.

SCHRADER, ELIZABETH. "Using Pictures To Help Slow Readers." *Grade Teacher* 70: 127; October 1952.

SHERMAN, MANDEL. "How To Use the Cross-Media Approach." *Teaching Tools* 5: 126-27; Summer 1958.

SPAULDING, SETH. "Research on Pictorial Illustration." *Audio-Visual Communication Review* 3: 35-45; Winter 1955.

SVEC, M. M. "Still Pictures." *Geographic Approaches to Social Education.* Nineteenth Yearbook. Washington, D.C.: National Council for the Social Studies, National Education Association, 1948. Chapter 13, p. 130-39.

TANNER, H. J. "Interpretation Through Pictures." *English Journal* 45: 277; May 1956.

THREATT, W. "We Learn Through Picture Study." *Instructor* 63: 37-38; January 1954.

UNDERHILL, C. S. "Sketch for a Picture Collection." *Wilson Library Bulletin* 30: 539-42; March 1956.

VEENENDAAL, WILFRED L. "The Visualization of an Idea." *Audio-Visual Instruction* 2: 260-62; December 1957.

VEGTER, D. O. "Using Still-Pictures in Geography." *Journal of Geography* 48: 334-36; November 1949.

VERNON, MAGDALEN D. "The Value of Pictorial Illustration." *British Journal of Educational Psychology* 23: 180-87; November 1953.

WATTON, H. L. "Study Prints Are To Study." *Instructor* 66: 17-18; January 1957.

WEAVER, GILBERT G., and BOLLINGER, ELROY W. *Visual Aids: Their Construction and Use.* New York: D. Van Nostrand Co., 1949. 388 p.

WILLIAMS, CATHARINE M. "Pictures with Purpose." *NEA Journal* 47: 196-97; March 1958.

WITTICH, WALTER, and SCHULLER, CHARLES. *Audio-Visual Materials; Their Nature and Use.* New York: Harper & Brothers, 1953. 564 p.

WYATT, A. "Developing Original Stories from Pictures." *American Childhood* 43: 15; January 1958.

Films and Filmstrips

Study Pictures and Learning. 58 frames, color. The Ohio State University, Bureau of Educational Research and Service, Teaching Aids Laboratory, Columbus 10, Ohio, 1960.

Teaching with Still Pictures. 53 frames, color. Basic Skills Films, 1355 Inverness Drive, Pasadena 3, California, 1958.

SOURCE MATERIALS

BROOKE, MILTON, and DUBESTER, HENRY J. *Guide to Color Prints.* Washington, D.C.: Scarecrow Press, 1953. 257 p.

GOINS, WILLIAM F., JR. "Life and Fortune Magazines as Sources of Science Pictures." *Science Education* 30: 10-11; February 1946.

KASS, BENJAMIN. *Complete Guide to Free Prints.* New York: Citadel Press, 1958. 115 p.

MILLER, BRUCE. *Sources of Free and Inexpensive Pictures.* Riverside, Calif.: the Author (Box 369), 1956. 35 p.

MILLER, J. L. "Some Picture-Story Books." *Elementary English* 33: 210-16; April 1956.

SUTTLES, PATRICIA H., editor. *Elementary Teachers Guide to Free Curriculum Materials.* Nineteenth edition. Randolph, Wis.: Educators Progress Service, 1962. 338 p.

SYRACUSE UNIVERSITY AUDIOVISUAL CENTER. *Instructional Materials for Teaching Audiovisual Courses.* Syracuse, N.Y.: Syracuse University Press, 1961. 74 p.